Melon

CW00358108

'One day. There you'll be, wa
always. One foot placing itsel
thoughtlessly, unwatchfully — nam above an, ...
front of another, strolling coolly along you are, possibly,
humming. Or humming eagerly along to where you go for your
pleasures, or because you're late for work, when suddenly — yes,
quite suddenly, without the slightest warning — the ground opens
at your feet.'

Melon is a successful publisher and ruthless patron of family,
friends and colleagues alike. In this acute and often very funny
examination of memory at work, he recalls the events which led
to his toppling. Published to coincide with its première, *Melon*
opened at the Haymarket Theatre, London in summer 1987.

SIMON GRAY was born in 1936. For twenty years he was a
lecturer in English Literature at Queen Mary College, London. He
has written a number of novels and television plays including
Sleeping Dog, Death of a Teddy Bear, for which he won the
Writers' Guild Award, *Pig in a Poke, Man in a Side-Car, Two
Sundays, Plaintiffs and Defendants, After Pilkington* and a
filmscript of J.L. Carr's *A Month in the Country.* Since his first
stage-play, *Wise Child* (1967), he has written *Dutch Uncle* (1969),
an adaptation of *The Idiot* for the National Theatre (1970),
Spoiled (1971) and *Butley,* which won the *Evening Standard* Best
Play award for 1971. *Otherwise Engaged* won both the *Evening
Standard* and *Plays and Players* Best Play awards for 1975.
Subsequent stage plays have been *Dog Days* (Oxford
Playhouse, 1976), *Molly* (Watford Palace, 1977; Comedy Theatre,
1978), *The Rear Column* (Globe Theatre, 1978), *Close of Play*
(National Theatre, 1979), *Stage Struck* (Vaudeville Theatre,
1979), *Quartermaine's Terms* (Queen's Theatre, 1981, the only
play ever to win the Cheltenham Prize for Literature), a version
of Molière's *Tartuffe* (Kennedy Center, Washington, 1982) and
The Common Pursuit (Lyric Theatre, Hammersmith, 1984, and
Long Wharf Theatre, Newhaven, U.S.A.; a revised version was
performed at the Matrix Theatre, Los Angeles in 1986, and
opened at the Promenade Theatre, New York on 19 October
1986).

SIMON GRAY

Melon

A METHUEN PAPERBACK

A METHUEN MODERN PLAY

First published in Great Britain as a paperback original in 1987
by Methuen London Ltd., 11 New Fetter Lane, London EC4P 4EE
and in the United States of America by Methuen Inc., 29 West
35th Street, New York, NY 10001.

Set in 10pt Journal by 𝍥 Tek Art Ltd, Croydon, Surrey.
Printed in Great Britain by Richard Clay Ltd, Bungay, Suffolk

British Library Cataloguing in Publication Data

Gray, Simon
   Melon. – (A Methuen modern play).
   I. Title
   822'.914   PR6057 .R33

   ISBN 0-413-16550-7

Acknowledgement
Melon was inspired by the book *Breakdown* by Stuart Sutherland,
expanded edition published by Weidenfeld & Nicolson, 1987.

CAUTION
All rights in this play are strictly reserved and application for
performance etc should be made before rehearsal to Judy Daish
Associates, 83 Eastbourne Mews, London W2 6LQ.
No performance may be given unless a licence has been obtained.

At the time of going to press, *Melon* was scheduled for first production by Duncan C. Weldon and Jerome Minskoff for Truimph Theatre Productions Ltd and the Shubert Organization Inc. During rehearsals of that production, instrumental music was replaced by singing. The cast was as follows:

Characters

MELON	Alan Bates
MICHAEL	Glyn Grain
GLADSTONE	William Squire
RUPERT	Tim Hardy
KATE	Carole Nimmons
JACOB	Sam Dastor
MELISSA	Donna Donovan
JOSH	Jason Carter
SAMANTHA	Shirley Cassedy
BARKLOW }	Jack Chissick
SIR ARCHIBALD }	

Directed by Christopher Morahan
Designed by Liz da Costa
Lighting Designer Robert Bryan
Musical Arrangement Stephen Oliver

The set. There is one set, consisting of four rooms. The psychiatric room, Melon's publishing office, Melon's bedroom and Melon's sitting-room. Ideally, the bedroom should be on a floor above, stage centre. I, for reasons I haven't bothered to clarify, have always seen the sitting-room as stage right, the office as stage left. The psychiatric room should obviously be up-stage, between the two. As this is a play about memory, there should be no scene breaks, each scene beginning almost before the previous scene has ended. It must be fluid, in other words.

The psychiatric room: Bleak. A chair, a table, the hint of a window perhaps. A wastepaper basket. Whenever the door is open, a glimpse of blackness.

The office: The room of a successful and busy publisher. A desk, intercom, and modern telephone system. Perhaps a sofa and an easy chair, as well as a functional chair behind the desk. As Melon is highly efficient, it should always be both orderly, and yet suggest that important things are in the process of happening. There are two doors. One, stage right, leads to the reception area. The other, stage left, leads to Michael's office, more a cubicle, which should be briefly glimpsed whenever he enters or exits.

The sitting-room: Entrance to it, as well as to front hall, and stairs to other rooms (i.e. bedroom) stage left. It is comfortable, well-used. There is the largest possible television set — possibly a faked up larger-than-available television set. In alignment with it, a sofa. Armchairs, a table, a desk, and possibly another sofa. Nice room, comfortable *and* elegant.

The bedroom: Two doors. One leading to the rest of the house, the other to an en suite bathroom. A double bed. A dressing-table and chair. As I've already indicated, it would be very good indeed if it could be on a higher level. Where sex usually takes place.

It would also be a good idea if playing space could be found Between the rooms, so that Melon is seen crossing and arriving, rather than just entering on stage.

ACT ONE

Scene One

Lights up on MELON *in the psychiatric room. Lights remain up in psychiatric room throughout play unless otherwise indicated.* MELON *sits in a chair.*

MELON. I'll tell you what happens. This is what happens. One day — one perfectly routine — perfect in its routineness, routine in its perfectness because one thing you discover when what happens — and it might! Why shouldn't it? That's the point after all — when what happens to me happens to you. You discover — (*Goes temporarily blank.*) — oh yes! that what is routine is perfection, the closest you can come to sheer perfection. And that it therefore follows as — as the day the — the night and the night the um day — that — the — other way round is true, too. Sheer perfection is routine. And routine is sheer perfection. (*Nods.*) But you don't know this, *won't* know this, until what happened to me happens to you. One day. There you'll be, walking along on the surface, as always. One foot placing itself casually, unthinkingly, thoughtlessly, unwatchfully — hah! above all, unwatchfully in front of another, strolling coolly along you are, possibly, humming. Or humming eagerly along to where you go for your pleasures, or because you're late for work, when suddenly — yes, quite suddenly without the slightest warning — the ground opens at your feet.

As he speaks, lights go up slowly on MELON's *publishing office.* MICHAEL *is sitting at* MELON's *desk, working.*

MELON *glances across stage towards office. He gets up, picking up briefcase, hurries towards office, stops.*

MELON. No, it's worse than that. The ground opens at a pair of feet which, *as it turns out, happen,* merely happen to belong to you. Merely happen — (*Laughs, nods, enters office, walking woodenly.*)

MELON (*seeing* MICHAEL). What are you doing there?

MICHAEL. Oh hello. I thought you weren't coming in.

MELON. There? At my desk?

MICHAEL. Well — I assumed you'd want me to finish off Agnes's cookbook for you. As it's got to go to the printers this evening. And you hate anything you're working on going out of the office — and as all your notes are here — and the proofs —

MELON *hasn't listened, gone to sofa, sat down.*

You're better then?

MELON. What?

MICHAEL. Sammy said you'd 'phoned. And said you were a bit under the weather. And wouldn't be coming in. You still don't look quite — quite yourself. What sort of weather have you been under?

MELON. It's a matter of digestion. Something I still haven't digested.

MICHAEL. Kate too?

MELON. Poisoned, you see.

MICHAEL. Poisoned? Kate?

MELON: No, me. Taken something rather poisonous into my system. That's all.

MICHAEL. Good God! Where did you eat last night?

MELON. At home. I ate a great deal at home. Cooked up by Kate and — and — (*Gets up, stares at* MICHAEL.) Nightmares. (*He trembles.*)

As he speaks, GLADSTONE *appears, goes towards door, opens it.*

GLADSTONE. Hello Mark, knew you'd be in, even though she

said you wouldn't.

MELON. Who?

GLADSTONE. Mmmm?

MELON. Who said I wouldn't.

GLADSTONE. That girl on the desk. Joey.

MELON. Who?

MICHAEL. Sammy. (*Looks at* MELON.) Sammy.

GLADSTONE. Mr Melon's never missed a day from illness, I said. He'll be in — that's odd. (*Staring at* MICHAEL.) Seeing you at Mark's desk. Creates a rather strange impression. Shakespearian.

MICHAEL. I'm just trying to get Agnes's cookbook off to the printers —

GLADSTONE. Mmmm?

MICHAEL. Agnes's cookbook! (*Little pause. Shouts:*) Agnes Merrivale's cookbook!

GLADSTONE. Oh, Agnes Merrivale's little project (*Peering.*) isn't it? So kind of you to have dreamed it up for her, Mark. To heal the breach. It's made her feel so much better about your turning down that last novel of hers. After so many years on our list. And I must say I'm relieved. Breaking the news that we couldn't afford to go on publishing her was one of my most unpleasant experiences. Most unpleasant. Have I ever told you about it?

MELON *lets out a crazed yap of laughter.*

Mmmm, well of course Mark's heard it before, haven't you Mark, but you hadn't joined us yet, had you, Michael?

MICHAEL. No. But you've told me, Arnold. Once or twice.

GLADSTONE. No, probably because I don't enjoy reliving it. She broke down, you know. And at L'Escargot too. That was the worst part. Because L'Escargot is where I always took her to celebrate every time she delivered a novel. So of course when I invited her there, she assumed it was for the usual celebration.

MELON. (*in a low wail*). Oh God! Oh God!

MICHAEL *glances at him alarmed.*

GLADSTONE. And I foolishly ordered champagne because that was part of the ritual too — and the waiter somehow managed to shower it over her hat, the moment after I'd told her we were turning her down. So she was in tears, you see — and there she was, dabbing away with her napkin at the champagne and at her tears, when old Bhgvadash Gupta came over, drunk as usual, and because it was the first day of spring, decided to serenade her with a song — (*Turns to* MELON.) — you know, Mark, that block I've always had about it either because I've tried so hard to remember or because it's so obvious, I suppose —

MELON, *who hasn't been listening, glances vaguely at him.*

— and last night it came to me, the tune as well, and of course Bhgvadash still had a strong Indian accent, and too drunk to notice Agnes's state, went right in — 'Oh Agnes, now that I see you so cheerful in one of your hats, my dear Agnes, I know spring has arrived.' (*Laughing.*) 'oh summer is icumen in, louder sing, cuckoo — cuckoo, cuckoo —'

MELON *leaps out of his chair, hurls himself on* GLADSTONE.

MELON. Oh you — you — oh you — (*Shaking* GLADSTONE *by the lapels.*)

MICHAEL. What are you doing, what are you doing? (*Pulls* MELON *away from* GLADSTONE.)

MELON. But he — he — you heard — he — (*Points at* GLADSTONE, *bursts into tears, lets out a wail, and begins to roll about on the floor.*)

He gets up shakily, dusts himself down and begins to walk towards psychiatric room, talking as he does. Lights up on psychiatric room. MELON *enters, still talking, lights having gone down on office.*

MELON. Now that wasn't — that wasn't a usual day at the office. For me. Not by any manner of means. For one thing, I don't make a practice of shaking the daylights out of harmless old bores (*Lets out a laugh.*) I mean, if I did, I'd have my work cut out, wouldn't I? There are so many of them around. Sometimes everywhere you look there's a harmless old bore. — And I don't go rolling wailing around on the floor like one of the Hashemite widows. I don't know why I said that — I don't know — I can't recall ever knowing — what a Hashemite is. Although I can guess how his widow probably behaves.

Lights begin to go up on MELON's *sitting-room.*

No, all I was trying to do was to pin down the moment — the exact moment when it started. When it became public. No longer possible to conceal the fact that the earth — the earth had opened — and the feet happened to be mine. But what they don't seem to understand, none of them, not *one of them* seems to have understood, though I go on trying to explain virtually every time they pop in to pop in a pill — (*Goes blank.*) — yes, what they've never understood is that there was a time when things were completely normal. For years and years. *Completely normal.* Take our regular Tuesday evenings, for instance. They were completely ours. Kate's and mine. Not just a part of our marriage, but a part — no, at the very centre — of *their* lives. Where would they have been without us? *That's* what I mean by normal. *More* than normal —

MELON *enters sitting-room, carrying a briefcase. He looks around. The TV is on. Earphones lie on the sofa, attached to the TV set.*

RUPERT *is on the TV.*

RUPERT. — the appointment of Mr Stan Barklow to the highly-sensitive post of atomic commissions supervisor has come as a surprise in government circles as well as beyond. I have Mr Barklow in the studio with me. Mr Barklow, you already have a considerable reputation as a man who lives up to one part of his name, you bark low. But if you had been born Stan Bitehard, you'd also have the reputation of living up to your name —

MELON *roars with contemptuous laughter, shakes his head.*

BARKLOW (*gently*). But I'm sure you understand better than most, Rupert, with your knowledge of what goes on behind the scenes in industrial relations, especially in an area like atomic reactors —

MELON (*laughs contemptuously*). Knowledge! Behind the scenes knowledge! The only behind the scenes knowledge he's got about anything is how to put on his make-up, you twerp! (*Turns the sound down, goes to his desk, opens his briefcase, takes papers out and from his pocket, a pocket calculator, and with an air of urgency begins to read the papers intensely but at great speed, while doing sums on the calculator.*)

During this, interview with BARKLOW *is followed by shot of football match.*

KATE *enters, towel around her, hair up, shampooed.*

KATE. Don't forget Lady Macbeth. She's waiting for you upstairs.

MELON. What? (*Stares at her.*)

KATE. Your son. Josh. He's Lady Macbeth in the school play, remember. He wants you to go through his lines with him.

MELON. Right. I'll be up in a minute, love.

KATE. Well, don't forget. (*Glances at TV screen where* RUPERT *has reappeared.*) Oh, look, there's our Rupert again. Who's he talking to? (*Turns up sound.*)

RUPERT (*on screen*). — now that you're through to the third round of the Cheeseboard Cup, Len, how does being a manager compare to being a player?

LEN (*on screen*). Well, Rupert, I know how closely you've followed the team this season —

KATE. Will he make it on time?

MELON. Oh, that's all taped. He'll be here. Could you turn him off, love? Something I have to read through before tomorrow and I've only got a few minutes.

KATE *hesitates as camera comes back to* RUPERT, *bends over, turns off set.* MELON *glances up at her, takes in her accidentally sexy posture.*

MELON. Mmmm. Very nice.

KATE *turns to him. They smile at each other.*

MELON. *Very* nice.

There is a ring at the doorbell.

MELON. Oh Christ! He's here. (*Looking at watch.*)

KATE (*in alarm*). Who?

MELON. Michael.

KATE. But it's not even half past six, I'm not even dressed — I haven't put the food —

MELON. No, don't worry, love, I asked him to come a bit early — I'll look after him. Let him in, will you, love? (*Still reading.*)

KATE. Like this?

MELON. He won't mind. (*Gives a little laugh.*)

KATE. But what about Josh?

MELON. You do it, love. Tell him I'm on for tomorrow evening.

KATE. Tomorrow evening he's on stage.

MELON *continues reading papers, working on calculator, as* KATE *exits.* MICHAEL *enters carrying a musical instrument.* MELON *continues reading, gestures a greeting.*

MELON (*still reading*). What did you think of Kate, eh?

MICHAEL. What?

MELON. In her towel. Thought I'd give you a little present.

MICHAEL. Oh. (*Little laugh.*) Thanks.

MELON (*still not looking up*). What is it about women in towels, or the right underwear? Stockings, suspender belts, slips shrugged on as if about to be shrugged off. (*Laughs.*) Who do they wear them for is the important question. Their husbands? Somebody else? Themselves? (*Laughs. Checks figures on calculator, signs papers, begins to put documents back in briefcase, puts calculator back into pocket. Bustles across to drinks counter.*)

MICHAEL. To tell you the truth, I've never found anything interesting in their clothes. Or underclothes. In my limited experience, granted that that's only Melissa — but even in films or magazines — oh, by the way, nothing for me, thanks, I'm on the wagon.

MELON. Is it confirmed that you're pregnant?

Little pause.

(*Laughs.*) Sorry, I mean, of course, that the two of you are about to have a baby, Melissa's pregnant, in other words. Is it confirmed? Kate said Melissa had 'phoned —

MICHAEL. Yes.

MELON. Congratulations. (*Hands him drink.*)

MICHAEL (*looks at it as if about to protest, doesn't*). Thank you.

MELON. If that's what you want, of course.

MICHAEL. It is. Really, we'd no idea how much we'd wanted a child until Melissa found out she was going to have one. Odd, isn't it? After ten years of fuss over coils, caps, pills, right back to condoms from the barbers, never failing to take precautions, we still can't work out how the fort was breached. But I suppose the unconscious need for a child —

MELON. No, no, listen. It's the other way round, the child's need for *you*. Think of the little buggers — the way they go at it from the second the testicles shoot them out — millions on millions in wave on wave. And tough and resourceful with it. It just requires *one* little bugger to make it up the tunnel and drill the target and bob's your uncle. Or Josh your son. Or whatever you're going to call him. (*Little pause.*) Or her.

MICHAEL (*laughs slightly*). Are you sure it works like that?

MELON. Absolutely not. Just putting it together from remembered sex lessons at school. But as you couldn't get O levels or A levels in it I didn't pay much attention.

MICHAEL (*shyly*). We thought we'd call it Jocasta if it's a girl and (*Slight hesitation.*) Marcus if it's a boy.

MELON (*after a pause*). Marcus.

MICHAEL. Not exactly after you. But somewhere behind you, Mark, with you in mind.

MELON. I'm touched. Or will be. If it's a boy. (*Laughs slightly.*) Melissa going to go on teaching?

MICHAEL. No. It's going to be a difficult pregnancy, apparently.

MELON. But afterwards? Going back to teaching?

MICHAEL. Not for a few years, at least, we've agreed. She wants it to have a proper childhood. So do I. In view of my own. I don't want to make the same mistake my parents made. Which was me. (*Laughs.*) Which means —

MELON. How are you going to live, then?

MICHAEL. Yes. (*Little pause.*) I know. I suppose I'll just have to try and get some more book reviewing until one of my novels finds a publisher — oh, that agent that nearly took me on — did I tell you —

MELON. What do you intend to do about accommodation? Battle it out in that bedsitter, the three of you?

MICHAEL (*after a slight pause*). Well, we can't really do that, of course, it's scarcely big enough for the two of us as it is. (*Laughs.*) Melissa's hoping her mother will come up with enough for a down payment on an unfurnished flat. Though so far she hasn't found the nerve — (*Shrugs.*)

MELON. I'm moving to Harkness and Gladstone, virtually taking it over in fact. In charge of everything. Made sure of that in my contract. First thing I'm going to want is an editor. I'll pay ten thousand a year and guarantee you some time off for your writing. (*Takes* MICHAEL's *glass in his hand, goes to drinks counter.*) Oh, I gave you a malt, didn't I, and you prefer straight scotch.

MICHAEL. No, I — (*As if about to reject drink altogether.*) — I'll stick with the malt.

MELON. Well, Michael (*As he pours drinks.*) about time you converted. What do you say? (*As he comes back with drinks.*)

MICHAEL (*taking his drink*). Well, it's generous, very generous of you, Mark — you're always such a good friend, unexpectedly good if I may — when it really counts — but I don't think — you see, I don't think — I'd have to talk it over with Melissa of course but she's already worried that I'm going to abandon what she calls my art (*Little laugh.*) — thinks I'd hold it against her. And the baby. — For the rest of our — our —

MELON. OK, Michael. There's no rush. Take the weekend to thrash it out with Melissa. And most importantly, don't fret too much on my account. Make your own decision, for your own sakes. I don't want even you if you're not committed, I've already lined up a second choice, she's a high-flyer only three years out of Oxford.

MICHAEL. She?

MELON. That's right. Some of them are very bright. (*Laughs.*) Like my wife, for instance. And she's pretty. Far prettier than you, now I come to think of it. (*Laughs.*)

There is a ring at the doorbell.

MICHAEL. Could I have until Wednesday?

MELON. Ah, that'll be old Rupe. Wednesday. (*Thoughtfully.*)

MICHAEL. Yes, we thought we might go away for a few days, you see. Somebody's lent us a cottage and if I can just get to the end of this draft —

MELON. Make it Tuesday.

Another ring at the doorbell.

Tuesday morning. I promised this girl I'd give her an answer by Tuesday evening and everybody's after her. (*Going towards door.*) Did you see Rupe, just now on the BBC or was it ITV, anyway, grovelling importantly away — to trades union leaders, football managers —

JACOB *enters, carrying a musical instrument.*

Good God, Jacob!

JACOB. Weren't you expecting me?

MELON. Frankly, no. I'd got out of the habit, you've been away so long. But I'm glad to see you, of course.

JACOB. Thank you. Michael, good evening.

MICHAEL. Jacob.

MELON. The question is whether we can cater for you. There's bound to be orange squash and probably apple juice in the kitchen – and of course Josh's Ribena, you were getting quite fond of that, weren't you?

JACOB. Actually, I'll have a whisky, please.

MELON. A whisky? Has something serious happened to you? Like developing adult tastes? (*Going to drinks counter.*) Malt or straight scotch?

JACOB. Either will do, thanks.

MELON. Really? In that case you get the straight scotch. Now let's get it over with. Fire away.

JACOB. What?

MELON. Tell us about Israel. (*Handing him a drink.*) What it's really like on a kibbutz, et cetera. Always sound as boring as hell to me, just like summer camp, with the fear of death thrown in. But I gather there's the sex. Although we got that in summer camp too. At least I did. In Somerset. Outside Yeovil. When I was fourteen.

JACOB *and* MICHAEL *look at him.*

What's the matter, am I being anti-semitic again?

JACOB. Yes, I think that must be it.

MELON. Oh, come on. Just because the idea of a kibbutz doesn't appeal to me –

JACOB. It doesn't appeal to me either.

MICHAEL. He hasn't been on a kibbutz. He hasn't even been to Israel.

MELON. What? Where the hell have you been then, these last six months?

MICHAEL. He's been in Australia. Melbourne. Working in a mental hospital. As a porter.

MELON. Is that right? Why as a porter?

JACOB. I thought I'd be more useful. And it meant I could get the patients to talk to me as if I were a normal human being. They

put on special acts for doctors, use a special vocabulary — they
see themselves as cases, you see. Some of the schizophrenics
especially —

MELON (*interrupting*). How does it make me anti-semitic? My
thinking you were in a kibbutz. In Israel.

JACOB. Oh, I suppose because you translated my going to
Australia to work with mental patients as my going to Israel to
work on a kibbutz. Because I'm Jewish. So you stereotyped
me.

MELON (*grunts*). Yes, I can see I stereotyped you to some
extent, i.e., Jacob away, now where did he say he was going?
Oh yes, somewhere hot, as he's a Jew it's probably Israel — but
the kibbutz part must be because I associate you with
dutifulness, always wanting to be useful, now that's not
anti-semitic, is it? Anti-semitic would be assuming you'd gone
off somewhere to set up as a tailor? Or as a money-lender?
Wouldn't it? (*To* MICHAEL:) So you're *assuming* my —
shorthand, is all it was really, is a manifestation of
anti-semitism because *you've* stereotyped *me*. Isn't it? Rather
offensively, if I may say so. In fact, *bloody* offensively.

JACOB *laughs, looks at* MICHAEL, *who smiles*.

What is it? What's up?

JACOB. Living among lunatics and Australians has made me
forget how violent conversation with a thoroughly sane
Englishman can be.

MELON. What do you mean? What does he mean?

MICHAEL. I think he's referring to your habit of — your need to
— win arguments.

JACOB. Actually, to your habit — or is it need? To create
arguments that you then need to win.

MELON. But it — *you* called *me* an anti-semite.

JACOB. No, I rather slackly accepted that definition. When you
offered it. What I suppose I took offence at is your not having
bothered to remember where it was I'd gone to. Especially as
we spent a good part of one of your Tuesday evenings

discussing it in this very room one Thursday just before I left. But I do fully concur that if I hadn't been a Jew, you'd probably have placed me in Australia. Or California. All right?

MELON (*thinks, nods*). Apology accepted.

JACOB *and* MICHAEL *look at* MELON. *Laugh.* MELON *also laughs.*

MELON. Hey, didn't Kate say something about your bringing around a new bloke? Half-chink or something, didn't she say?

JACOB. Actually he's half-Indian.

MELON. What's the other half?

JACOB. Irish.

MELON. Well why didn't you bring one half or the other. Both halves, if you wanted.

JACOB. Yes, well — thanks. (*Taking drink.*) As a matter of fact I've lost him. Mislaid him, anyway. We were coming back from *Rigoletto* last night, and there was a group of Canadian students going to investigate some doss-house they'd heard about in East Finchley. He decided to join up with them for a bit. He's rather — friendly, you see. At least with other people. Unfortunately I had too much dignity to accompany them. Or not enough nerve. They were wearing shorts. With rucksacks on their backs.

MICHAEL. Oh, I'm sure he'll turn up.

MELON. Really? Why?

JACOB. Yes, why? The only reason I can think of is that he likes his creature comforts. I feed him well, provide him with hot baths, the use of a telephone, so — there's some hope. (*Little laugh.*) Sometimes I wonder why I bothered to come out of the cupboard.

MICHAEL. Don't you mean — um — closet?

MELON. Yes, Jake, now you're back, do try and get our idioms right. We keep our skeletons in the cupboard and our queens in the closet.

JACOB. You know, Mark, I sometimes think it isn't all an act, you actually do have it in for gays.

MELON. Oh come on, Jake, I've told you often enough. The only thing I've got against you is you put the part of the body I most admire into the part for which I have the least respect. Anyway it's only sex.

JACOB. Yes, only sex. By the way, I've been offered a job — a partnership actually.

MELON. With a firm of shrinks, I take it?

JACOB. No. It's just a group practice in the Mile End Road, as a matter of fact.

MELON (*incredulously*). The Mile End Road!

JACOB. Yes, the Mile End Road. I've decided I'll be more useful there, you see.

MELON. Useful? Dishing out aspirins while you listen to them whine on about their jobs, their lack of jobs, their illegitimate babies, their wife-battering husbands, their sex-denying wives — wouldn't it be more useful to use your brain? Since you've got quite a good one.

MICHAEL. Do you mean you're giving up psychiatry?

JABOB. Not altogether. There's a clinic in the neighbourhood and they've agreed to let me be involved, in some capacity or another.

MELON. What — you mean as a porter?

JACOB. If necessary.

MELON. Christ, Jake! Well, it's your life. If you want to spend it aspirin-peddling and loony-spotting down in the East End — just as long as you're not going in for some moral martyrdom, to make up for being queer —

KATE *enters sitting-room.*

Oh hello, love, when did you get that, I like it. (*Gestures to dress.*)

KATE. Last year. I thought I'd go on wearing it until you noticed it.

MELON. Then your patience has paid off. How are you taking it tonight, tonic or lime?

KATE. Tonic, please.

MELON *goes to drinks table.*

MELON. You've missed the best part of the evening, as usual. Which always happens before it properly begins, eh? I've offered Michael a job, and we've been thrashing out Jake's personal problems.

KATE. In characteristically delicate style, I'm sure.

MICHAEL *and* JACOB *laugh.*

MELON. That chink — no, Indian, half-Indian, half-Irish you promised me he was bringing has run off with some Aussie — no, Canadian hitchhikers.

There is a ring at the doorbell.

MELON. Oh bugger, there's Rupe.

KATE. I'll go. (*Exits.*)

JACOB. Look, Mark — do you think — would you mind — not going into that particular aspect of my life in front of Rupert?

MELON. Which particular aspect?

JACOB. Actually, any particular aspect. But particularly the sexual —

KATE *and* RUPERT *enter,* RUPERT *carrying a musical instrument.*

MELON (*casually*). 'Lo Rupe, old bean, usual triple malt?

RUPERT. No, just tomato juice, please.

MELON. Really, why? (*As* RUPERT *exchanges nods, smiles with* MICHAEL *and* JACOB.)

RUPERT. I'm taking it easy for a while. Can't afford to get jowly —

MELON. Oh, I don't know. Caught you on telly this evening, with a nuclear trades unionist and a football manager, seemed to me a bit of weight was just what you needed. In your interviews, anyway. And I don't see where else you could put

it. Except on your face. As that's all you let us look at. And
so. Who have you fucked this week? (*Looks around.*) Well he
always finds ways of letting us know, last week the Russian
ballerina who defected, the week before the Turkish novelist,
the week before that — I forget, but anyway, somebody he'd
interviewed that either needed to be fucked badly or badly
interviewed —

KATE. Darling!

MELON. What's the matter, love?

KATE. I sometimes wonder why anyone puts up with you.

RUPERT. Or how.

MELON. Oh, you mean because I happen to say exactly what
comes into my mind.

KATE. It's partly that. And it's partly what comes into your
mind. That you then say.

MELON. Nothing that doesn't come into most people's minds.
The *only* difference is my saying it. And as to how and why
people put up with me —

KATE. Well?

There is a ring at the doorbell.

MELON. Who the hell can that be at this hour?

KATE. It must be Melissa.

MICHAEL. Melissa. (*Blankly.*) Good God, yes, of course. I'd
completely forgotten. Because she came separately. (*Going
to door.*) I'll let her in.

MELON. Come on, Rupe, you still haven't answered my question.

RUPERT. Actually, do you mind if I have a malt after all? Just a
dash of malt.

MELON. Just a dash — Christ, Rupe, what's the matter with you?
I ask you a simple question and you behave like a pick-pocket
who's suddenly discovered he's at the policemen's ball. And
you're the bloke who on one famous occasion at college —
remember — (*To* MICHAEL *and* JACOB:) took out a list from

his pocket and read off a dozen names, as if announcing the
prize-winners —

RUPERT *(to* KATE): Congratulations, by the way.

MELON. What? What for?

RUPERT. Somebody at the BBC just told me that you're going
up from script editor to producer.

MELON. Really? *(To* KATE:) Why didn't you tell me?

KATE. I didn't want to tell anyone. Until it's confirmed.

   MICHAEL *enters with* MELISSA *who is carrying a musical
   instrument.*

MELON. What — *(Taking them in with surprise.)* oh, it's you.
   love. Don't worry about being late. As nobody noticed you
   weren't here anyway. Not even your hubby. So you're harry
   preggers —

   MELISSA, *who has been attempting to smile, bursts into
   tears.*

MELON. What's the matter? Have I said something?

   They look at MELON, *the look seeming to become cold and
   accusatory.*

   MELON *stands for a moment, then turns, hurries through into
   the psychiatric room. Sits down, puts his hand to his face.*

MELON. Of course I can see — in retrospect. Looking back, that
   is. I don't deny — can't deny — that I was sometimes
   somewhat lacking in — in — that I was sometimes rather over
   — um. But it was only — only — my manner. And also, don't
   forget, it's me — me myself is telling. *(Stops.)* It's I I self that
   am telling — myself am telling. Remorselessly. And in fact,
   also inaccurately. At my own expense. Because of course
   that wasn't any special evening, any particular evening, but a
   sort of flavour of an evening, and years ago. Years and years
   ago. I mean, certain things did happen — for example offering
   Michael a job, and Jacob's return from Israel, and teasing —
   Rupert about his sexual adventures. *(Stops. Lets out a wild
   laugh. Checks himself.)* Australia. Oh God! Yes, well — and
   Melissa of course — but they didn't all happen together really.

On the same evening.

During MELON'*s speech, the others have been chattering in
low voices, sociably.* RUPERT *takes out his musical
instrument. Begins to play.* KATE *gets hers. Begins to play.*
JACOB, MICHAEL, MELISSA *join in. They play very softly.*

Of course not. It's just that when I look back on an evening,
everything like that seems to have happened together, and so it
makes me seem worse. Even worse. To myself. Than I in fact
was. And it is true. Absolutely true. And it was Jake who
hinted — well, said as much. That they were fond of me. *Were*
my friends. Apart from one. Or possibly two. As it turned out.
But they were my friends *then*. And I did lead them, I was the
— the harmonizing spirit. However odd that may seem to other
people. Or even myself sometimes when I look back. I was the
— the — (*Turns, looks around, picks up his instrument, goes
over, joins in, playing a different piece of music, with great
confidence, insisting on it, and so rapidly imposing it on the
others, until they are all playing* MELON'*s tune. They all
continue to play, low, as:*) — principle of harmony. For years
really. For years and years. Um. I lead the band, orchestrated
the — the essential sound, developed the counter-points and
— and so forth.

The music rises again. Suddenly slightly discordant.

MELON *frowning, continues playing, attempts to impose his
tune. The music goes lower, still slightly discordant.*

Which is not to say that there weren't occasional discords.
Things slightly off. Just — just enough to set one's teeth on
edge. But that was inevitable. From time to time. After all, we
were all getting on with our own lives, in between — and
generally — generally I succeeded in imposing the right — the
right noise.

MELON *plays more emphatically. The slight discord
continues.* MELON *stops playing abruptly. All the others stop
playing, but one after another, gratingly until only* KATE
*continues to play, dreamily. One by one the others pack up their
instruments and leave, gesturing goodbyes.* KATE *continues to
play.* MELON *watches her, then plays with her for a short*

time. They are now alone. He stops. Watches her again.
KATE *stops playing, continues to gaze, abstracted, as music goes on without her.*

MELON. We didn't, of course, any of us, actually play any musical instruments. It's just that when I first began to talk about — explain what had happened between us all, I found myself using it as a — a metaphor, and one or two of them didn't quite understand it was a metaphor, and so it became something that actually happened — I mean I remembered our playing, heard our playing, saw it. So even when I remember the evening when some of them claimed it all began. When they say that if only I hadn't — I hadn't — then none of the rest of it would have happened — even that evening has been changed by them, because of my accidental — accidental but *apt* metaphor — into a musical evening. Ridiculous. That that's how I remember it . . .

He watches KATE *for a moment, who is continuing to play softly and dreamily throughout this.*

KATE *sees him watching her, stops playing, gives an odd little laugh. Puts her musical instrument away,* MELON *watching her very closely.*

MELON. There was an odd note this evening. Somebody off key, I thought. Did you catch it, love?

KATE. No. I thought there was rather a nice feeling. Relaxed and lively. Perhaps because *you* were quite soft, for once. And didn't insist on keeping the glasses full.

MELON. No, somebody was off, all right. I had an idea at first it was Jake, worn out with his East End aspirin-pushing and looney-coddling.

KATE. He just looked lonely, to me. As usual.

MELON. Wonder why he can't hang on to any one.

KATE. He's too desperate. It shows. It puts them off.

MELON. And it couldn't have been Rupert, of course.

KATE. Why not?

MELON. The only false note from Rupert would be a genuine one. He's just one loud false note. His career. His fucks. (*Gestures, dismissively.*)

KATE. Still, I wish you wouldn't show him your contempt.

MELON. He doesn't notice.

KATE. I suspect he does, sometimes.

MELON. Good! Then I haven't been wasting it, have I? (*Laughs.*)

KATE. Well, that leaves Michael. Or Melissa. Issuing forth your false notes.

MELON. The only note she's issued since that baby was born —

KATE. He's not a baby any more. He's three. And he's called Marcus. After you.

MELON. Then ever since Marcus was born as a baby, the only note she's issued behind that perpetual smile is something between a whine and a sob. That's all he hears at the moment. The whine of his wife, becoming the whine of his life. And as for him, poor bugger, I didn't hear anything I don't hear every day at the office. Nothing false there.

KATE. Well, that's everyone then. Except yourself.

MELON. Everyone except myself except yourself, love. And it's not myself, because if it were, I'd have identified myself straight off, wouldn't I? So that leaves yourself. And now I've worked it out I realize I've been hearing it, off and on, on and off, quite a lot recently, when we've been by ourselves alone.

KATE. And what is the false note you've been hearing.

MELON. Fidelity.

KATE (*after a small pause*). Do you mean *infidelity,* by any chance?

MELON. That would be the true note.

KATE. I see. And that's *not* coming from you?

MELON. Oh yes. Yes it is. The true note of infidelity has come from me for a long time, as you know. I've never made much effort to conceal my little adventures from you, have I? And recently less and less so.

KATE. I've certainly suspected you of lying recently, if that's what you mean.

MELON. I know. But my lies have just been a kind of courtesy, haven't they, love? Not really even an intention to deceive.

KATE. Thank you for the courtesy. And for not intending to deceive me.

MELON. There's no need to deceive you. As they're not important. Just —

KATE. Little adventures.

MELON. Exactly. But your infidelity is different. Altogether more serious. That's why I've been hearing your false note. You've *intended* to deceive me. You've *minded* my finding out.

KATE. And do you mind your finding out?

MELON (*after a pause, intensely*). I love you.

KATE. Do you want me to stop?

MELON (*carefully*). Does having an affair make you happy?

KATE. It's —

MELON. Go on, love.

KATE. It could be perfectly acceptable. Under the circumstances. What do you feel about it?

MELON. Oh — (*Little pause.*) as a matter of fact I feel — I feel — (*Hoarsely.*) excited. Bloody excited.

There is a pause.

KATE (*nods*). Excited?

MELON. Yes. I don't know why, really. (*Little laugh.*) After all, it's perfectly usual — conventional even these days. Having what's called an open marriage, eh?

KATE. Yes, of course. That's what it's called, isn't it, what we have?

MELON. What we have *now*. From this minute forth. Well — well — (*Gets up, walks around, comes back, looks at her.*) Who is it, your bloke? Your other bloke?

KATE. Oh, nobody of much consequence, really, I'm afraid. Sorry, darling.

MELON. Have I met him?

KATE. Not that you'd have noticed.

MELON. You'd rather not tell me his name?

KATE. Do you need to know it?

MELON. Funny thing is — funny thing is I'd rather not know it.

KATE. Then don't worry, darling. I shan't tell you.

MELON. Thank you.

KATE (*smiles*). May I now — (*Puts her hands up, lets her hair down.*)

> MELON *holds out his hand to her. Raises her up. Begins to undress her.*

MELON. I want you to know that — I shall always love you.

KATE (*looks into his eyes, smiles*). Thank you.

MELON. Knowing you — and not knowing you — makes you even more beautiful. You see?

KATE. There's nothing more to me than there ever was.

MELON. There's a secret between us. We share my not sharing it with you. You're my wife. And yet you've become separate again. To be wooed. But still entirely mine. Already possessed. Just like a bride. (*Begins to undress her, only just controlling his excitement.*)

KATE (*touching him*). And yet you make me sound a bit like a prisoner, after all.

MELON. How can you be? When you can keep such an important part of your life to yourself. Which is why I don't want you ever to tell me. Even when it's over.

KATE. If it's ever over.

> MELON *looks at her.*

KATE. I can still give him up. If you want me to.

MELON. When you've just given me such a perfect answer. It was like an electric shock. Right through my system. (*Continues to undress her.*) Nevertheless, there's one thing — one thing only — I need to know about him. What he's like physically. But only in the most rudimentary terms. Whether he's tall or short, blond or dark, Jew or gentile, bow-legged or straight-limbed?

KATE. Yes.

MELON *laughs in triumph, pushes her to the bed, and as he continues to undress her:*

KATE. Assuming, that is, that he's a he.

MELON *stops, stares down at her, then kisses her passionately.*

Lights down on the bedroom.

MELON *steps out, straightening his clothes, goes towards psychiatric room where lights have come up.*

MELON. And that's all there was to it. Not important to either of us at all. Although of course the conversation wasn't really like that, not as compressed, not as neat, not as final. It was an — (*Thinks.*) open conversation. But because they attached such importance to the whole business, and particularly to how it began, they made me go through it again and again.

Lights up on MELON *sitting-room.*

And again. Sometimes two or three times in a session. Like policemen. So that it is now unshakeable. Police testimony. Parrot testimony. About my own life. That they then offered in evidence against me again and again and again. And all it really amounted to — in spite of their charge sheet, their evidence, my testimony against myself, their prosecution, their persecution — all it amounted to was I'd found an itch, you see.

KATE *enters through front door, goes into sitting-room, carrying briefcase. She sits down, opens case, puts on glasses, takes out papers, begins to read and make notes.*

Just a delicious itch to scratch at when I felt in the mood. It gave me a little extra something for years and years without doing anyone any harm. (*Stops, suddenly bellows.*) I loved my wife! (*Little pause.*) Love my wife. There isn't anybody else. There's never been anybody else. Just her. (*Staring at* KATE, *lovingly*.) To love.

JOSH *enters sitting-room, with a yoghurt, which he is eating.*

MELON *stares at him in momentary shock as he realizes he's forgotten* JOSH.

MELON (*recovering himself*). I mean apart from — apart from — (*Looks towards* JOSH *again.*)

KATE *beckons* JOSH *over for a kiss, then* JOSH *goes to sofa, turns on television, puts on earphones.*

KATE *resumes working.*

MELON *goes through front door, down hall, enters sitting-room. He goes over and kisses* KATE, *his attention fixed on* JOSH.

MELON. And what have you been up to, this evening? Eh Josh?

JOSH. Over to Yaki's.

MELON. What's that, a strip club?

JOSH. A Japanese.

MELON. Japanese strip club?

KATE. A Japanese friend, darling. From school. What did you do, darling?

JOSH. Oh, nothing much.

MELON. I've always wondered how you do that? I mean, does it require special equipment?

JOSH. No, not a thing. (*Channel hopping at great speed.*)

MELON. Do you talk?

JOSH. Talk?

MELON. Yes. Talk.

JOSH. What about?

MELON. Oh, the state of the world. The bomb. Sudden death. Tolstoy. All the little perplexities that besiege us.

JOSH. No.

MELON. Why not?

JOSH. They never seem to come up.

MELON. Really? Never seem to come up, the world, the bomb, Tolstoy and sudden death?

JOSH. Not with us.

MELON. And what's Yaki going to do?

JOSH. When?

MELON. When he grows up.

JOSH. He is grown up.

MELON. Afterwards, then.

JOSH. He's thinking of becoming a policeman.

MELON. Good God! You mean a Japanese policeman!

JOSH. Well, he's already Japanese. All he has to do is to become a policeman.

MELON *fumes quietly*.

KATE. I think your father meant a policeman in Japan.

MELON. Acutally, I meant in England. Hence the Good God! At the prospect of a Japanese policeman in England. Good God!

KATE. Yes, well — which is it?

JOSH. Don't know. Depends on whether he goes back to Japan or stays here, I suppose.

MELON. Why a policeman in either country?

JOSH. I expect the money's good, eh?

MELON. Ah. Well, I'm glad he's got his eyes anchored firmly on the ground.

JOSH. You mean his little slant eyes?

MELON *says nothing*.

KATE. I think I'll go to bed.

MELON. Right, love. Right. Join you in a minute, love.

KATE *goes out, upstairs, into bedroom, where lights go up faintly. She begins to get undressed then exits through door to an en suite bathroom as:*

MELON. And why should you think I meant his little slant eyes?

JOSH *shrugs*.

Why should you think I meant his little slant eyes, Josh?

JOSH (*shrugs*). Sorry.

MELON. Why should you think that's what I meant?

JOSH. Well, I suppose it's the kind of thing I've heard you say.

MELON. About Japanese?

JOSH. Well, about anybody. You don't mind what you say. As long as it's true. I've heard you say.

MELON. Would you mind turning off that bloody machine?

JOSH *does*.

And allow me the privilege of seeing your face when we talk.

JOSH. Sorry. I didn't know we were talking.

MELON. What did you think we were doing?

JOSH. Having an exchange.

MELON. Yes — well. I would just like to clear up some of the implicit accusations contained in your side of the exchange, if I may. With your help. Is it your belief that I show contempt for the physical characteristics of individuals or races?

JOSH. *Show* contempt?

MELON. Am contemptuous of.

JOSH (*thinks*). I don't know.

MELON. Really? But then if you don't know, you shouldn't attribute. Should you?

JOSH. No. Sorry.

MELON. And what are his eyes like, Taki's?

JOSH. Yaki's.

MELON. Yaki's, what are his eyes like?

JOSH. Like most Japanese.

MELON. And how would you describe the eyes of most Japanese?

JOSH. I don't know. Black, I suppose.

MELON. Large or small?

JOSH (*shrugs*). Small, I suppose.

MELON. And are they on the horizontal, or do they slant?

JOSH. Slant, I suppose.

MELON. Exactly.

JOSH (*after a pause*). Exactly what?

MELON. I — um — (*Suddenly bewildered.*) yes. Well, what I'm getting at — my point is that — (*Stops again.*) that I hope you grasp that there's a difference between (*Gathering coherence and confidence.*) a crude and quite irrelevant reference to racial characteristics and simple descriptive accuracy. When I referred to Taki's — Yaki's — little slant eyes I was being, by your own admission, absolutely spot on, wasn't I?

JOSH. But you didn't refer to his little slant eyes. I did. And then attributed the description to you. It was all my fault. For starting this. Sorry.

MELON. Yes, yes, that's right. I got a little — you have a way of tangling me up in myself sometimes, Josh. You're the only person in the world who can do that, you know. Tying me up in my own knots. Blood knots they must be, eh? (*Laughs.*) Well — why not bring him around here sometime. Let me have a look at him eh? And your mother? (*Little pause.*) I mean, let your mother have a look at him. *Both* of us have a look at him. (*Laughs.*) What did you say he wanted to be?

JOSH. A policeman.

MELON. A policeman. Yes. That's right. For the money, wasn't it?

JOSH. Yes. For the money.

MELON. Well, I assure you I haven't got anything against policemen either.

JOSH. I have.

MELON (*makes to speak. Checks himself.*). Well, we'd better not get into that one, eh, or in no time we'd be into CND, the bomb, American air bases, setting a moral lead versus requiring a deterrent to negotiate, so forth, we'd still be here at six in the morning, and then where would we be?

JOSH. Here, I expect.

MELON. What?

JOSH. If we were at it at six in the morning, I expect we'd be at it here. Or in the kitchen. (*Little pause.*) You were asking where we'd be.

MELON *bangs his fist down on his knee.* JOSH *looks at him in surprise.*

MELON. Yes well — (*Laughs. Bangs his fist down again with an appearance of heartiness.*) Time I hit the sack. What are you going to do? (*Getting up.*)

JOSH. Oh just mess about down here.

MELON. When's your first A level, exactly?

JOSH. Oh, not until (*Thinks.*) tomorrow morning.

MELON (*stares at him*). Oh. A joke. I see. (*Laughs.*) Well — anyway, don't be too late, will you?

JOSH. No, daddy.

MELON *exits, looks back.* JOSH *has turned television back on, taking a pack of crisps out of his pocket, begun eating them, while*

MELON (*stares at* JOSH, *then steps away*). Yes, well as they say, hostages to fortune, eh? The thing about Josh — old Josh and myself is that — that — Josh and I have always had a rather — a rather — we've always — respected each other's positions. In the sense that. (*Stops.*) Of course they made a great deal out of the fact that we didn't — I didn't always fully open myself to his problems. But how could I, if I didn't know what the problems were? And if I didn't it could be because he didn't have any problems, couldn't it? As I tried to point out. Just because *I* have problems doesn't mean that my son has problems. Apart from me. That I admit. For a time I was a problem. But possibly his only problem. But I couldn't open myself up to discuss his problem with him if I was in fact his problem, could I, because the kind of problem I was was precisely the kind of problem that couldn't be talked to, let alone talked to about. (*Little pause.*) Right?

KATE *comes out of bathroom in nightdress, goes to bed, sits on it, puts on glasses, picks up book, but doesn't actually get into bed. Her posture is distinctly sexy.* MELON *looks towards bedroom as if able to see her.*

MELON (*his gaze still on* KATE, *continues*). But in my heart I knew – I've always known – that Josh was his own self.

JOSH *has stopped eating crisps, has drawn up his knees, and is sitting hunched, as if in despair.*

MELON *glances vaguely at him, then:*

Without any need for my – need for my – (*His attention goes back to* KATE.) Besides there was this other thing – (*Goes to bedroom.*) – that soon became permanent. My itch. (*Stands in bedroom, looking at* KATE.) My – delicious, my delightful, my tormentingly insatiable itch – that needed and needed and needed (*Thinks.*) to be scratched.

Lights still up on JOSH, *huddled on sofa.*

MELON (*to* KATE): Tell me. (*Goes to bed, sits down.*) Your bloke. Does he like a hand inside your thigh? (*Doing it.*)

KATE. Yes, he does.

MELON (*his other hand touching one breast, then the other*). And which of your breasts does he prefer?

KATE. He likes them both equally. So he says.

MELON. And does he like to kiss – (*Bending his head towards her breast as* KATE *puts a hand on his head.*) – does he like to kiss them? (*Kisses each breast.*)

KATE. Yes, he does.

MELON. In other words – (*He stands up and looks down at her.*) he dares to do everything that I do.

KATE. Yes.

MELON. Does he (*Hesitates slightly.*) – does he do more?

KATE (*smiles.*) Come to bed.

MELON (*hesitates.*) No. More. Does he do more?

KATE. More? I don't know.

MELON (*after a short pause*). Well, I'll just have to make sure he can't.

KATE. And how will you do that?

MELON. By doing so much more myself, that there's nothing left for him to do.

KATE (*smiles*). Come to bed.

> MELON *looks at her, seems suddenly uncertain, turns, goes through en suite bathroom. Lights remain up on* KATE, *low on* JOSH *still on sofa, as* MELON *walks, lost, back to the psychiatric room. Stands, staring at* KATE.

MELON. But it was just an itch. That's my point. Nothing more than that. I mean just a part — a small part —

> *Lights come up on* MELON's *office.* GLADSTONE *is standing at desk, looking agitated.*

— of what was going on in my life. Busy life. My busy life. My active life. So full of quite other things. (*Looks towards office, looks towards* KATE.) Not just itches and scratches and sex as they've tried to make out. That's all *they* could understand — (*As lights go down on* KATE *and* JOSH.) I had my work. (*He goes towards office.*)

> MELON *enters office full of buoyancy.*

GLADSTONE. Good morning, Mark.

MELON (*cheerfully*). I'll give you three minutes, then you're out on your arse.

GLADSTONE. Mmmm?

> MELON *goes to telephone, picks it up.*

MELON (*on telephone*). Sammy, tell Michael to come and see me in a couple of minutes. (*Puts telephone down.*)

GLADSTONE. I won't detain you. I know how much you always have to do. Just wanted to make a little report on my supper

with Agnes last night. It was nothing like as fraught as you
feared it would be, and she *is* such a marvellous little cook,
you know, always a dab hand at light meals, snacks, however
simple the ingredients she always contrives to make them taste
and look exotic, she really is a creative spirit, even in adversity
— but alas I did indeed get the *cri de coeur* you warned me I'd
get, though you were wrong about her having a new novel up
her sleeve, or reverting to the question of your having let the
old ones slip gracefully out of print, what she wanted to know
was might there be anything, any *little* thing we might
commission from her, she suggested a garland of her favourite
verse, which she thinks could go well in schools, though
perhaps her taste is too much with the Sitwells, or, more
interestingly, she wondered about a travel book, preferably of
her beloved Dordogne, with one or two of her water-colours in
illustration, or indeed was there *anything we* could propose.
Well, there you are. I said I'd pass it on to you.

MELON. I might let her do our new homosexual sex manual.

GLADSTONE. Well, any little thing, I promise you she won't
be too fussy — oh, there *is* one other thing, Mark. That young
man you brought in specifically to assist you.

MELON. If you mean Michael, Arnold, he's been with us for
nearly five years.

GLADSTONE. Oh yes, I do agree. And of course now that you're
managing editor, with complete authority, and the support of
the board whenever you need it, so I wouldn't dream of
questioning any of your appointments — but I have to tell
you, Mark, that I'm not alone in finding his manners at our
general editorial meetings quite alarming. Must he — must he
really debate quite so ferociously while remaining completely
inaudible? Please correct me on this, Mark, but the only thing
of his I heard distinctly or distinctly thought I heard yesterday
morning was his suggestion that we should launch a
homosexual sex instructions manual, can that be right?

MELON. Time's almost up, Arnold.

GLADSTONE. Yes. Well I'm dismayed, yes I admit dismayed
that it should even pass through his mind that we'd give our

imprimatur to such a project A quite unnecessary one, I
also happen to think, as I'm perfectly sure that those who
prefer to practise homosexuality know perfectly well how to
do whatever it is they do do without instructions and diagrams
from the publishing house of Harkness and Gladstone, at least
they did in *my* day, good grief, Mark! And another thing,
Mark, it's not only his demeanour and general tone that
distresses me —

MICHAEL (*enters*). Oh. Morning, Arnold.

GLADSTONE (*unaware*). — but there have been rumours
circulating about his unpunctuality, his general laxness, and
even his drinking. The idea of his actually *drinking* — here — in
the office —

MELON (*bellowing*). I'll have a word with him, Arnold!

GLADSTONE. Mmmm?

MICHAEL. With whom?

MELON. The janitor. He's been boozing in the cellar again.

GLADSTONE (*taking* MICHAEL *in*). Well — well I must up to
my little eyrie. There to fashion in cunning and exile, eh? And
if you can think of something for poor Agnes — (*Gives a
cursory nod to* MICHAEL.)

MICHAEL. How are the memoirs going, Arnold?

GLADSTONE *hurries out with a gesture.*

MICHAEL *stares after* GLADSTONE, *turns to* MELON.

MICHAEL. My usual reception. (*Gives a bitter laugh.*) You
wanted something?

MELON. Yes, I wanted you to get old Bore out of my room, so I
can get on with my work. Thanks. (*Takes calculator out of his
pocket, keys in rapidly figures on a sheet in front of him.*)

MICHAEL. You mean he left simply because I showed up?

MELON *grunts affirmatively.*

MICHAEL (*after a slight pause*). Look, what has he got against
me?

MELON. Does it matter? Old Bore's of no consequence except as an old bore. And an old nuisance.

MICHAEL. It happens to be of consequence to me.

MELON (*sighs*). OK. What he's got against you immediately is your proposal of a homosexual sex manual.

MICHAEL (*gapes*). Homosex — but that wasn't me. That was you.

MELON. You bet it was. And don't worry, I'll take the credit for it when the time comes.

MICHAEL. Then what's going on?

MELON. It's quite simple. If he doesn't like something I'm doing he pretends he thinks you're doing it, and then comes to me and abuses you for it.

MICHAEL. But why?

MELON. Because he wouldn't dare abuse me, of course.

MICHAEL. So I've become his — his whipping boy, is that it?

MELON. That's it.

MICHAEL. And you think that's all right?

MELON. I think it's bloody marvellous. It means I don't have to waste time and energy going through the motions of arguing with him. Under the terms of my agreement with Harkness and Gladstone I'm stuck with Arnold William Hewitt Old Bore and Old Nuisance Gladstone virtually 'til death do us part. So I can either throw him out of the window, a solution which crosses my mind about twice a day every day of my life or devise humane strategies to keep him out of my hair. Why do you think I sicked him on to writing his memoirs? So he'd spend most of his time up in the attic, grovelling about for records of lunches with Ezra, teas with Tom, pints with Dylan, cocktails with Wystan —

MICHAEL *goes to pour himself a drink.*

MELON *watches him.*

Everything all right at home?

MICHAEL. Yes, fine. Why shouldn't it be?

MELON. You said the other day Melissa was having trouble with the nursery school. Because Marcus had taken to kicking little girls. Or something.

MICHAEL. Oh, it isn't just the little girls, it's the other little boys and the teachers too. Of course the joke is Old Bore and I agree about practically everything. The books he doesn't want you to publish I don't want you to publish either, and the books he's ashamed of our publishing I'm ashamed of too — (*Raises glass to lips.*)

MELON. Do you really need that?

MICHAEL. I don't know but I want it. Why?

MELON. It could be the reason that you've started mislaying things. Forgetting to answer letters. Arriving late. Leaving early for the pub. Even Old Bore has been hearing things. But particularly about your drinking. It could mean trouble, Michael.

MICHAEL. But Old Bore doesn't matter. As you've just pointed out.

MELON. What matters is that your work is beginning to suffer.

MICHAEL. Work! You call what I do work! (*After a little pause.*) You know what I hate most about what you've done here, that for the most part we don't even put out honest-to-God crap, for people to read on trains or planes or in the lavatory. We just process commodities. That happen to come in book form.

MELON. Fortunately a lot of people seem to think our commodities useful. (*Working on his calculator.*)

MICHAEL. What you mean by useful is that they make a profit.

MELON. I certainly mean that too, because if they didn't we wouldn't get our wages, would we? And I find mine bloody useful. Don't you?

MICHAEL. Harkness and Gladstone had a great list once. And a tradition. A long tradition. Then you came.

MELON. It had a long overdraft too. It was just about to go under, tradition, list and all. Then I came.

MICHAEL (*drinks*). At college you said you wanted to be a writer.

MELON. Yes, I've been waiting for you to bring that up. I lied. At college what I wanted was to be like the rest of you. But I matured into wanting to be successful instead. Which I am. Unlike the rest of you.

MICHAEL (*nods*). Tell me why you wanted me to join you. To be your professional conscience? Is that it?

MELON (*in an American accent*). Listen kid, I want a professional conscience like I want a boil on my ass.

MICHAEL. Then why? As somebody you can patronize, whose intelligence you can ignore, whose instincts you can despise — just one of the trappings of your success? Is that why you need me, Mark?

MELON. It's true I'm very fond of you. Always have been. But I don't need you, Michael. Never have.

MICHAEL. I resign.

MELON. You won't. You haven't got the guts. You can't survive without your job here. You're not going to cut it as a writer. You haven't got the talent. Or the will. Or the luck. Or the right wife. Or whatever writers need to cut it. You haven't any choice but to cling here as long as I'll let you, wallow in your martyrdom, pick up your pay-check, and take it home to your Melissa, whom in your turn you can't abide, to help nourish your Marcus, whom in your heart you can't stand. And I'll only let you as long as you don't drink in the office. Or turn up here drunk. Or late. Or get careless. (*Hands him a pile of envelopes.*) Now hand these to Sammy on the way out. Tell her I want them posted this evening, there's a good boy.

MICHAEL *stands as if about to throw the envelopes into* MELON'*s face. Brings himself under control, smiles.*

MICHAEL. Posted this evening. (*Nods.*) Right. (*Goes towards door,* MELON *grinning at him.*)

MICHAEL *turns.*

MICHAEL. Oh, by the way, people say you know who it is.

MELON. Know who what is?

MICHAEL. Kate's bloke.

MELON. Really? What people?

MICHAEL. Oh you know, just people. People one bumps into who know you. Or have heard about you.

MELON. Really? Then they're wrong.

MICHAEL. You're right. Sorry. What they say is that it's somebody you know, not that you know who it is.

MELON. Then they're wrong again. If it's somebody I know I'd know who it is, wouldn't I?

MICHAEL. Would you? (*Nods.*)

MELON (*disturbed, looks as his desk*). Oh, would you mind giving some envelopes to Sammy? Tell her to post them this evening — (*Looking for them.*)

MICHAEL. I've got them. (*Shows them.*) See you this evening, then.

MELON. This evening?

MICHAEL. Yes. For one of your Tuesdays.

MELON. Today's Thursday.

MICHAEL. Exactly.

MELON (*after a moment*). Oh, of course. (*Laughs.*) Right. See you this evening.

MICHAEL *gestures, wags the envelopes at him, goes out through to his office.*

MELON. No, no, that never happened. Never happened. At least not like that. Not that sort of brutal — brutal — (*Begins to get undressed.*) It's just that they've gone on and on so much about our relationship, Michael's and mine, that I really do believe that they've lodged their view of my view of it in my mind so that my view of it has finally become their view of my view of it. One of them actually claimed that I looked forward to a confrontation with him as one might — might look forward to a sexual encounter with a woman — how did it go? How did he put it? — with a woman one was determined never to have sex with because looking forward to the sex was far more fun than having the sex itself. So that really he was just another (*Thinks.*) itch. Yes. Itch. For me to scratch. The point I was trying to make — the point I was making was about my work. What they called ruthless, overbearing, opportunistic, I called — I call — I *know* — was just efficient, ambitious and hard-working. Yes, above all, hard-working. And by God, how hard I worked. I worked and worked. Because that was an itch too. Another itch to scratch. Perhaps even my main itch.

SAMANTHA *knocks, enters, holding papers.*

SAMANTHA. Oh. You're in a hurry then? As usual.

MELON. What? (*Takes in his state of undress.*) Oh, yes, poppet. It's the evening for one of our evenings. (*Crosses to the door, locks it.*)

SAMANTHA. I thought your evenings were on Tuesdays.

MELON. That's right, poppet, Tuesdays.

SAMANTHA. Today's Thursday.

MELON. Of course it is. I generally know the day of the week, as well as the time of day, you know, poppet.

SAMANTHA. Then you also know that as it's a Thursday evening you don't have to get back for one of your Tuesday evenings.

MELON. Yes, I do. We're holding them on Thursdays at the moment.

SAMANTHA. You're holding Tuesday evenings on Thursdays?

MELON (*now down to underpants*). Just until Kate's finished her current production. Then we'll go back to holding them on Tuesdays. Until her next production. When it'll depend which evening is free for our Tuesdays, evening. It's a matter of tradition, we've been holding our Tuesday evenings for years, and we're not going to stop simply because we can't have it on Tuesdays, what the hell are we talking about this for, anyway, why aren't you getting undressed?

SAMANTHA. I was hoping you'd go through my Coriolanus with me.

MELON. Haven't the time, love. I'll try and fix it early tomorrow. Here. Come on. (*Begins to undress her.*)

SAMANTHA. Do you promise?

MELON. Yes. No, come to think of it, the way the traffic's been buggering me up this week, but some time during the next two days, OK?

SAMANTHA. But that's no good. I've got to hand it in tomorrow morning. And I only got a B-question-mark-minus on my Macbeth.

MELON. Yes, well the problem is I've never believed in those bloody witches. If they'd asked me to write on the usual crap, ambition, self-murder, treachery, that lot, we'd have been home and dry. Got rid of the minus at least. And probably the question mark. And don't forget our B-plus on Lear — what are you doing? (*As* SAMANTHA *bends to undo her stocking.*)

SAMANTHA. Oh sorry. (*Moves away.*)

MELON. Where are you going?

SAMANTHA. Haven't you time for me to pour myself a drink, at least?

MELON (*glances irritably at his watch*). Help yourself, love.

SAMANTHA *pours drink.* MELON *sits down on edge of sofa. Glances down at essay.*

In sitting-room, lights come up and down, up and down, like blinks, in which we see KATE *embracing an unidentifiable man.*

MELON, *as if suddenly aware of this image, stares towards it. It continues briefly to flicker, then black.*

MELON *stares at blackness, blinking. Puts his hand to his forehead, looks down at the essay. Looks towards room again, then sees* SAMANTHA *who is pouring herself a drink and is standing watching* MELON *as she sips it.*

MELON. What the hell are you doing?

SAMANTHA. Observing you.

MELON. Why?

SAMANTHA. Because sometimes you look quite sweet. When you're just sitting around in your knickers being quiet, instead of bowling about all over the shop, being dynamic and blustery. (*Coming over to him, sitting on his lap.*) What do you think?

MELON. The first paragraph isn't bad. Not bad at all. You haven't been cribbing again, have you?

SAMANTHA. Of course I haven't. Ever since you warned me —

MELON. What am I going to do if you get into your bloody college?

SAMANTHA. Poke my successor. Or one of the secretaries. (*Rumples his hair.*) The new tea-girl wouldn't mind a go.

MELON. Really? The West Indian? How do you know?

SAMANTHA. Because I heard her saying she fancied somebody rotten. And who else could that be but you?

MELON (*laughs*). Come here, poppet. (*Takes her in his arms. They kiss enthusiastically, then* MELON *slides down her body, proceeds to kiss the patch above her stocking tops.*)

Lights come up and down on sitting-room. KATE *in a state of undress.* MAN *leaning in a posture of sensual worship, his hands on her body. As:*

SAMANTHA. Why do you always do that?

Lights go to black in sitting-room.

MELON (*blinking*). Because I've got a religious streak in me. And this is the nearest I can get to ritual. (*Begins to slide down her knickers as he finds himself staring towards blackness.*)

Lights flicker up and down as before on KATE *and* MAN.

Blackout on both rooms.

Act Two

Lights up on MELON's *office.*

MELON *is sitting in his chair, dressed, staring towards sitting-room, which is dark. Lights on in bedroom, turned on by* KATE, *as she enters, wearing a very attractive evening dress. She stretches, yawns, sits down on edge of bed.*

SAMANTHA (*now dressed, picks up her essay*). Well, I'm ready.

MELON. Ready? Oh — (*Looks at his watch.*) well, we'd better be quick, I've got to get back —

SAMANTHA. I know. It's Thursday, so it's Tuesday evening.

MELON. That's it. (*Begins to undress, stops. Looks at her.*) But we've just — haven't we?

SAMANTHA (*after a little pause*). You really don't remember?

MELON. Yes, yes, of course I do, love (*Laughs.*) It's just that — something happened. A strange — something happened. In — in my — (*Points to his head.*) in there. Very odd. (*Little laugh.*)

SAMANTHA. You mean a black-out? But that's serious. You should see someone. Even a doctor.

MELON. No, no. Not a black-out. Quite the opposite. Pictures. Very vivid. As if they had been loitering about in the back of the skull, and then suddenly — (*Gestures.*) sort of stepped forward. Grinning. (*Glances towards bedroom again.* KATE *lets out a little laugh of remembered pleasure, stretches again, goes into en suite bathroom.* MELON *shakes his head.*) I'm all right now. But why did you say you were ready then? That's what confused me.

SAMANTHA. I meant I'm ready to trot off now. Like a good girl. And no, I won't forget to post your letters and no, I won't forget to put the answering machine on, and no, I won't forget to set the security alarm, and yes, tonight is the night for the cleaners, they always come on Thursday even when it's Thursday.

MELON *looks towards room again, then turns to look at* SAMANTHA.

MELON. You all right, poppet?

SAMANTHA. Fine. I'm fine. It's just that sometimes I wish —

MELON (*glancing towards bedroom again*). Wish what?

SAMANTHA. Oh. That I was having an affair with my boss.

MELON. What? Oh — (*Laughs.*) you'd hate it. All the fuss and feelings. This is much better. Now trot along, poppet, like a good girl, and don't forget to set the answering machine — (*Stops, shakes his head.*) um — don't forget that tomorrow we'll eliminate the minus. And the question mark, eh?

SAMANTHA. You know — perhaps you ought to have a check-up or something. You're not yourself. (*Hesitates.*) And the sex —

MELON. What about the sex?

SAMANTHA. You didn't enjoy it.

MELON. How do you know?

SAMANTHA. Because there wasn't enough of it to enjoy. For the first time ever. (*Exits.*)

MELON. What they called my sexual harassment, my abuse of power, my abuse of my own sexuality, treating women as objects. But just because I have — have always had a perfectly easy, matter-of-fact, healthy liking — yes, that's the word — healthy. And relaxed. And good. It made me feel good. And why shouldn't it? Along with everything else it was a workout, exercise that brings into play all kinds of muscles you don't use on the tennis court, and even some — certainly one — you don't use in swimming. At least not usually. Depends who you're swimming with, I suppose. (*Barks out a laugh, stops, momentarily bewildered.*) But what is wrong, can be wrong, with doing something that a) does you good and b) doesn't do anybody else any harm?

He stares towards bedroom.

KATE *comes through door of en suite bathroom, in nightdress, climbs into bed, puts on glasses from bedside table, picks up paperback, tries to read, loses concentration, puts paperback down on her stomach, hands underneath her head, clearly thinking.*

I've never given or contracted a venereal disease. Never given or contracted herpes. Never given or contracted Aids, by God — I've always been clean, chosen clean partners, done it cleanly! (*Shouting.*) So what's wrong with having a good scratch every so often. All right, often and often and whenever I could. It's not my fault that I itch most of the time! And what harm have I done? I haven't given Aids, herpes, vener — (*Stops. Stares.*) Sometimes I feel as if I've spent the last however long it's been in the dock, struggling to preserve my reputation, my liberty, my — my very life itself. But don't they know, surely everybody knows these days, even the medical profession must know, that it isn't actually a crime, it's not necessarily one's own fault. I didn't make the ground open. It could have opened at anybody's feet, yes, even at their's.

MELON *is staring towards* KATE *as he speaks. He now runs out of psychiatric room, across stage to bedroom, as if to commit a violence. He enters bedroom.*

KATE. Coming to bed, darling?

MELON. Something wrong, something odd, about the evening. I thought. Did you notice it, love?

KATE. No. I thought everybody was really rather — jolly.

MELON. You mean they drank a lot. (*Laughs.*)

KATE. Hardly their fault, darling. The rate at which you filled the glasses. Nice to see Jake looking positively happy, do you think David might actually become permanent —

MELON. I thought his name was Donald.

KATE. No darling, David.

MELON. He told me Donald. I'm sure he did. He smelt funny, Jake.

KATE. Did he? Oh — perhaps his shampoo. He ought to wash his hair more often, it gives it such a glow. I do wish Josh would put in an appearance, if only for a few minutes. People would love to see him.

MELON. What, giving his impersonation of a deaf-mute, you mean? Or perhaps he really has turned into a deaf-mute. As he never speaks, it's hard to know — oh, by the way, what was going on between you and Michael, love?

KATE. Me and Michael?

MELON. Yes. Early on. When you were whispering together. In the kitchen.

KATE. Oh. Yes. He was telling me about Marcus. He's in trouble for bullying again.

MELON. But why the whispering?

KATE. Well, it's not something Michael's likely to announce at the top of his voice, is it, darling? And he didn't want Melissa to know he'd told me. She's ashamed. He's at his wit's end —

MELON. There was something — something — perhaps it was Rupert. How did Rupert seem to you, love?

KATE. Fine. A little subdued perhaps. Apparently his ratings are going down —

MELON. Yes, yes, I know that. He never stopped talking about it — what always surprises me is that people turn him on, not that they turn him off — no, it wasn't that — it was — it was — that business with the book, for instance. I couldn't make it out.

KATE. What book, darling?

MELON. That book that turned out to belong to him. The Memoirs of Sir Archibald Mc something. Twain. Sir Archibald McTwain. It turned out to be his, Rupert's.

KATE *looks at him.*

MELON. Odd book for Rupert. Of all people. And it seemed —
something about the way he left it. As if he were stealing it.
Embarrassed by it. I don't know.

KATE *continues to look at him.*

MELON (*looks back at her*). I don't know.

KATE. Come to bed, darling.

MELON. And also — something else. I've never known you look
quite so extraordinary. So extraordinarily (*Swallows.*) good to
look at.

KATE. You liked my new outfit then, did you?

MELON. It was ravishing. Yes, ravishing. At least it — ravished
me. The truth is, love, I couldn't take my eyes off you all
evening. Wherever you went, whoever you talked to, my eyes
followed.

KATE. Ah, there you are then. That's what was odd. Or wrong.
You.

MELON. Your eyes sparkled, as if — (*Takes off her glasses.*) They
still are sparkling, love.

KATE. Are they?

MELON. Is it because — because you saw your bloke this
afternoon, love?

KATE. Or it could be because I'm seeing him now.

MELON. But — but you did see him this afternoon, your bloke,
didn't you?

KATE *nods.*

I seem to have got this idea — from somewhere. Somehow.
That I know who it is. No, I mean that it's somebody I know.

KATE *says nothing.*

Is it, love?

KATE. That's not for me to say.

MELON. Why not, love?

KATE. Because you don't want me to. You've always insisted I'm not to. More fun. You've said.

MELON. Right. Yes, that's right. (*Gives a laugh.*) It's just that I've had some rather funny moments recently. Unexpected sensations. Odd glimpses of this and that. In the brain. Sleeping badly, nightmares —

KATE. I know, darling. I've heard you cry out. My poor darling. You've been working too hard. You always do. So come to bed and I'll send you to sleep.

MELON (*abruptly*). Is he a bit of a wag, your bloke, love?

KATE (*laughs*). My bloke love?

MELON. No, love. (*Impatiently.*) Your bloke. Is he a wag?

KATE. I find him quite amusing. Why?

MELON. Well that was another thing about this evening. You were full of jokes. Almost every time you spoke somebody laughed. I don't mean you don't normally make jokes. But these were different.

KATE. You mean they were funny?

MELON. For instance, when you described the head of plays, I think it was, as an old queen who wouldn't come out of his cupboard, wasn't that it?

KATE. No, I said it to Jake. About Jake. Not the head of plays. We were reminiscing, you see, darling, about the time years ago when he said something about having come out of the cupboard at last and you said the cupboard is where we keep our skeletons, we keep our queens in the closet.

MELON. Oh. Did I?

KATE. So it was just your own waggishness you were noticing. From when you were in your prime as a wag.

MELON (*after a pause*). Well, what sort of jokes does he make? Your bloke. Give me a — a feel of them.

KATE. I'd rather not.

MELON. Why not?

KATE. Oh — I suppose because they'd merely sound crude. Out of context.

MELON. Well, put them in context.

KATE. The context is usually pretty crude, too.

MELON (*laughs, in spite of himself*). Is that him? I mean, his sort of joke?

KATE (*lightly, smiling*). I didn't mean it to be a joke.

MELON. What does he vote?

KATE. He's undecided.

MELON. Between what?

KATE. Between Liberal and SDP.

MELON. What does he do?

KATE. Do?

MELON. His work.

KATE. You can't ask that. It's against the rules.

MELON. You've never approved of this, really, have you? This game?

KATE. I've never said that.

MELON. No, but once you said it was like pornography. It excited artificially.

KATE. Did I? I don't remember ever —

MELON. We could stop now, if you wanted.

KATE (*after a little pause*). How would we stop?

MELON. Oh easy. All you have to do to stop it is to tell me who it is. Then there'd be nothing left for me to guess. Would there?

KATE. I'd rather go on as we are.

MELON. But why, love?

KATE. I've become used to it. You've taught me to become used to it. I prefer it this way.

MELON. Very well. Then — then vouchsafe some fact. Any true fact about him. I don't mind how trivial it is, as long as it's personal.

KATE. No, I can't do that. You have to ask. Those are the rules.

Your rules.

MELON. I *am* asking.

KATE. No, you're not. You're begging. You have to ask a question. And I have to decide whether I'm willing to answer it.

MELON. Is he — is he younger than me?

KATE. You're of an age, almost.

MELON (*quickly*). And tell me —

KATE (*interrupting*). No more questions. Not now. Keep some back for tomorrow and tomorrow and tomorrow. Come to bed. You've made me itch, isn't that what you always call it, itchy? Yes, you've made me really very itchy, darling. (*Holding out her arms.*)

MELON (*standing*). It's not me that's made you itchy. It's him. Talking about him. Thinking about him. Remembering him. Isn't it, love?

KATE. Ah. But it's you I want to scratch me, darling. Come to bed. (*Pleadingly, erotically.*)

MELON *stands looking down at her, in a kind of shock as: Blackout.*

Sound of MELON *and* KATE *making love. Cries of ecstacy, sighs, snores, silence.*

Lights up brilliantly on MELON *sitting-room.* MELON *is standing in the middle of it, as loud ringing on doorbell, simultaneously door opens,* JACOB *enters.*

JACOB *stands for a moment, then bursts into tears.*

MELON. What's the matter?

JACOB. It's Daffyd. (*Sniffling.*)

MELON. Daffyd? Donald, don't you mean? As in Donald Duck. (*Makes quacking noise.*)

JACOB: That's right. Donald. He's left me. He says I smell like a dog. A freshly shampooed dog.

MELON. And you do. Musty and sweet. Feral. Noticed it myself.

But no need to take it personally. (*Going to drinks bar.*) Just change your brand and find somebody else — (*Pouring out an enormous goblet of malt*) is my advice to you, speaking as a sane, outspoken Englishman, here, take this.

JACOB (*takes goblet, drains it down*). Where's Josh?

MELON. Oh no. You stay away from my boy. I'm not having you put the part of you I least admire into the part of him I most respect, he can't help being a deaf-mute, Jake.

JACOB. Kate then. Where's she?

MELON. You stay away from her too, Jake. I'm not having her screwed by a Jew.

> JACOB, *finishing goblet, looks at him.*

Queer, I mean. She can be screwed by a Jew any day of the week, but getting herself screwed by a queer would make me look bad. I have my pride.

JACOB (*picks up book*). What's this? The Memoirs of Sir Archibald McTwaddle. Have you seen the pictures? (*Laughs.*) Sir Archibald at Sandhurst, Sir Archibald at the Western Front, Sir Archibald at the Palace, Sir Archibald at his wife's funeral, Sir Archibald with the companion of his later years, the spaniel Archie, Sir Archibald and Archie at the Royal Opera House —

MELON (*takes book from him, after a slight tussle*). Enough of that, Josh, if you please, sir. (*Laughs.*) Here, give me your glass.

JACOB. No, no, really, one goblet is enough —

MELON. Nonsense. You're in the house of an Englishman. Hospitality Melon's my name — (*Wrestling glass from him. Going to bar.*) — not to talk of nature. Sane and sensible with it. How are your loonies, still gobbling down aspirins on the National Health?

Violent ring on the door.

(*Pouring another full goblet of malt.*) Hah, old Rupey-doop-doop! (*Doing a shimmy, singing name.*) So who've you been fucking today, doopy-rupe-dooooop? (*Singing, shimmying, his back to door as:*)

MICHAEL (*entering*). Your wife as usual.

    MELON *freezes. Turns. Looks at* MICHAEL.

MELON. My wife?

MICHAEL. Yes.

MELON. You mean Kate?

MICHAEL. Yes. (*Gravely*.) I'm sorry.

MELON. Why? Wasn't she any good? (*Laughs*.)

    MICHAEL *and* JACOB *laugh.*

MELON (*wiping away tears of laughter*). So you're turning into a
    wag too, Mik-hay-el? I don't know how they'll take that in
    the office. Where you're known as old sober-sides. Even when
    you're drunk. Which you mainly are. (*Laughs*.)

    MICHAEL *and* JACOB *laugh.*

    What'll you have to drink?

MICHAEL. Orange squash mixed with ribena, and a dash, just a
    dash of tobasco. Really light on the tobasco.

MELON (*mixing drink*). Coming right up.

MICHAEL (*picks up book*). What's this? Hah! Archibald McTosh,
    Memoirs of. (*Laughs*.)

MELON (*turning, quietly, dangerously*). Do you mind putting
    that down? I don't know how it managed to get into my
    home, but I can't bear the sight of it. It's an interloper.

MICHAEL. You're the boss. (*Putting it down*.) Even I wouldn't
    want to publish it. (*Laughs*.)

MELON (*brings back drinks*). Here you are. (*Slapping goblet into*
    JACOB's *hand, diminutive sherry glass into* MICHAEL's.)
    Down the hatch. Both of you. Go!

    They drink.

    Where's misery-mugs? Coming separately, as usual?

MICHAEL. No, sir.

MELON. Why not?

MICHAEL. Because we've separated.

MELON. What, rid of misery-mugs at last, well done!

JACOB. Yes, congratulations, Michael, my dear. (*In Jewish accent.*)

They laugh, toast each other.

MELON. But what about the little bugger your son, don't tell us you're stuck with him.

MICHAEL. Not. If I. Can help it.

JACOB (*in Jewish accent*). That's my boy!

MELON. Well done, sweetie-pie. This could mean – (*pause.*) promotion!

MICHAEL. Oh thank you, thank you, Marcus!

JACOB. Yes, thank you, thank you, Marcus, my dear.

MELON. But I warn you, don't you go trying to steal my Lady Macbeth from me.

MICHAEL. Your Coriolanus, don't you mean. We all know she's yours, Marcus.

MELON. Wonderful body, simple soul —

JACOB }
MICHAEL } — question-mark-minus-mind.

MELON. On Thursdays.

JACOB. On Tuesdays.

MELON. On Thursdays and Tuesdays.

JACOB. On Tuesdays on Tuesday.

MELON. Yes, but on Thursdays, Tuesdays.

JACOB. Today is Tuesday.

MELON. Yes, but falling on a Thursday.

JACOB. Tell him, my dear.

MICHAEL. Today Tuesday falls on a Tuesday.

MELON (*shouting*). Nonsense! Rubbish! Today Tuesday falls on Thursday. As ever.

MICHAEL (*quietly*). Tuesday on Tuesday.

JACOB. Tuesday on Tuesday. That's today. Tuesday. (*Lisping, heavily Jewish.*)

MELON (*looks at them both, containing violence*). Tuesday on Tuesday, Tuesday on Thursday, you lay off my poppet, got it!

The bell rings violently.

RUPERT *enters, a fraction before it's finished ringing.*

MELON. Ah, Rupert, what can I get you to drink, malt — (*Trails away as:*)

RUPERT *goes straight to the bar, makes himself an enormous and complicated drink while humming.* MELON *stands watching him indignantly.*

MELON. Make yourself at home!

RUPERT. Thanks, cock. Where's the lemon?

MELON. Lemon?

RUPERT. That's right, Melon cock. Where's the lemon?

MELON (*strides over, seizes lemon*). Here it is! Right under your bloody nose! Here's the lemon, cock.

RUPERT. Thanks, cock. (*Slices it up.*) Of no consequence.

MELON. Who?

RUPERT. Decently average. Decently intelligent. Decently pleasant person.

MELON (*shouting*). Who?

RUPERT. The woman I fucked today. (*Lifts glass.*) Thank you cock. (*Drinks it down.*)

MELON *watches* RUPERT *as* RUPERT *dabs at his mouth.*

RUPERT. Too heavy on the tobasco. Not your fault, cock.

MELON. What does she look like?

RUPERT. Who cock?

MELON. The woman you fucked today.

RUPERT. Oh, she has a smile of such radiance, cock, such
delicacy of speech, a manner so — so enigmatic —

MELON. I said what does she look like! I'm talking legs, tits,
bum —

JACOB. Yes, that's right. He is. Legs. Tits. That's what he's
talking, Rupe.

MICHAEL. And bum. What's her bum like, Rupe?

MELON. That's what we want to know. Legs. *And* tits. *And* bum.

MICHAEL. Legs have priority.

JACOB. No, tits. Tits are special. Even I —

KATE *enters. She is wearing high-heeled shoes, stockings, a
suspender belt, in a parody of a soft-porn pin-up. A towel
around her head.*

MELON (*claps, whistles*). Wow! Yipee! Look at her! Now d'you
see what I mean! That's my girlie!

As KATE *adopts a number of erotic postures:*

Hey, poppet, not too close to Jake, he might throw up, eh?
(*Laughs, claps at another posture,* MICHAEL *joining in
whole-heartedly,* JACOB *fastidiously.*) That's enough, poppet,
you come over here, by Daddy, like a good girlie.

KATE *saunters over, stands by him.*

MELON (*to* RUPERT, *gloatingly*). How does she measure up to
this? (*Little pause.*) Your decent woman. Eh. cock?

RUPERT (*blithely*). Don't know, cock. I've never seen her like
that. Wouldn't want to. Prefer her naked. Smiling her radiant
smiling while I listen to her enigmatic —

MELON. Hah! But what's she like when you come to it, cock?
Does she give you a good itch, itch, itch, that you can scratch,
scratch, scratch, as my poppet does. (*Putting arm proudly
around* KATE.) Eh, poppet?

RUPERT. Actually, she's quite exhausting, thank you for asking,
cock. But then so am I. We leave each other completely wrung
out.

KATE (*suggestively*). Like a — pair of — washing machines, you mean?

RUPERT. Like a pair of washing machines, poppet and cock. We leave each other completely wrung out. But — (*Seeing book.*) what's that?

MELON. So that bloody thing's yours, is it? I might have guessed.

RUPERT. Certainly not, sir. Surprised, not to say astonished, to find the blighter in your home, cock sir. (*Makes to pick it up.*)

MELON. Then don't touch it, Rupert. I warn you. (*With great intensity.*) It's vicious. And pornographic. I'm going to burn it when you've gone.

There is a pause.

MELON (*falling into a confusion as he see faces around him, staring at him*). Now what — where — who — you were telling us something, I do believe, was he not, love?

KATE (*reverting to* KATE's *usual manner*). Nothing much, really, darling. Because what he wants to tell us, he's leaving out. (*To* MICHAEL *and* JACOB:) Isn't he?

MELON. What's he leaving out? What are you leaving out? (*Stares at* RUPERT.)

RUPERT. Why, the obvious thing. That's what I'm leaving out, cock. Aren't I?

OTHERS. Yes exactly, the obvious thing! (*Etc.*)

MELON. And what's that?

RUPERT *gestures to others, as if leading a choir.*

OTHERS. He loves her! (*In unison.*)

RUPERT. Exactly. I love her, cock. (*Little pause.*) That's what I'm leaving out. But you wouldn't understand that. Being what you are.

OTHERS. Being what you are.

MELON (*after a little pause*). And what am I?

MICHAEL. Oh, we can't tell you that.

MELON. Why not? (*Little pause, slight laugh*.) Am I too complicated, too darkly etched, too subtly shaded —

JACOB. On the contrary, Mark. Too simple. A single word would cover you.

OTHERS. A single word.

JACOB. But I can't tell you what it is, you'd take dreadful offence, Mark.

OTHERS. Dreadful offence!

MELON. Crap! Crap, I say! I'm a simple, straightforward, sane Englishman. I never take offence. Give it, but never take it, is virtually my motto.

MICHAEL. But you'd take offence at this word. If you're any sort of man, Mark.

MELON (*to* RUPERT): Come on then!

RUPERT. Oh no. I couldn't. After all I'm a guest in your house.

MELON (*to* KATE): Do you know what this word is?

KATE. Yes, darling. I do, I'm afraid.

MELON. Then out with it!

KATE. Oh, I couldn't. After all, I'm a guest in your house too, in a way. I mean, we're all guests, even in our own houses. My old nanny used to say.

MELON (*turns away, as if to speak generally, turns back to* KATE.) You never had an old nanny. You never had any sort of nanny.

KATE. But if I'd had one, that's the sort of thing she'd have said, darling. (*To others*:) Wouldn't she?

OTHERS. She would. Yes. (*Etc.*)

MELON. Then it's bloody lucky you didn't have one, love. Or you'd have gone around saying some bloody stupid things, wouldn't you? Now come on, I want this word, so let's have it, one of you. Or all of you.

MICHAEL. Why don't you try and work it out for yourself? You're good at working things out for yourself.

OTHERS. That's right. Work it out. For yourself.

MELON. All right. I will. (*Takes an old-fashioned abacus out of his pocket, begins to work it.*) Now I need some facts. Give me some facts.

JACOB. You know all the facts.

OTHERS. Yes, you know all the facts —

MELON. But I don't know the big fact, do I? Which is what I am. According to you lot.

KATE. Of course you do, darling. You know all the facts. Big and little. Doesn't he?

OTHERS (*murmur*). Of course, darling. Yes, darling (*Etc.*)

MELON. Then what am I doing with this? What am I trying to work out?

RUPERT. The word that covers the facts. That's all. The name for it.

MELON. Well, do I know this word? Do I know this name?

KATE. Of course you do, darling.

RUPERT. Everybody knows it, cock.

JACOB. Everybody.

MICHAEL. It's perfectly obvious.

KATE. A child could work it out, darling.

MELON. Then why can't I?

KATE. Well, you're not a child, darling.

RUPERT. You lack a child's innocence, cock.

MICHAEL. And his wisdom.

JACOB. Not to mention his quickness of mind.

MELON. All right! All right! I've had enough of this! (*Throws abacus on floor.*) What is it, this word, eh? Let's have it, this word of yours.

KATE. But darling. It's your word. It describes you. Not us.

RUPERT. And you know what you are, cock. As well as we do. Better even.

MICHAEL. You boast about it.

JACOB. Flaunt it.

RUPERT. You'd announce it on television, cock if I gave you air-time.

KATE. So you see it's only the word itself.

MICHAEL. A little matter of the word itself.

JACOB. Yes, one disgusting little word itself.

RUPERT. And what does that matter, darling?

JOSH *enters.*

MELON. Josh, you know this word?

JOSH. I'm a child, aren't I? I guessed it easily.

KATE. Come on, darling, think.

OTHERS. Think! Yes, think!

MELISSA *enters, dressed exactly as in Act One, but enormously pregnant. She is weeping.*

MELON. Well, about time you showed up, this word we're talking about, that people use of me, what is it, come on, misery-mugs out with it, let's have it.

MELISSA *looks at him, makes to speak, bursts into shrill laughter, runs out of the room.*

OTHERS *laugh, applaud, 'Good old Melissa.' 'Good old misery-mugs.' Etc.*

There is a silence.

MELON. All right. All right. I give up!

KATE. I don't believe it.

RUPERT. Nor do I.

MICHAEL *and* JACOB *shake their heads.*

MELON. Don't believe what?

KATE. You've never given up in your life.

MICHAEL. No, you don't give up on anything. Does he?

JOSH. Never, daddy. You're always telling me. 'Never give up.' Remember. 'If at first you don't succeed.' Remember. Robert Bruce and the spider. Alfred and the cakes. Patty cake and the baker's man. Li'ul Jack Horner, dada. (*Voice becoming more infantile*.) Wemember, wemember, the fifth o' September . . .

MELON. November, twerp. Fifth of November!

JOSH *cries.*

KATE. So have another go, darling.

RUPERT. Yes, go on, darling.

MICHAEL. Yes, darling. Another go.

JACOB. Please darling, try.

JOSH. For my sake, darling.

MELON (*after a pause, pathetically*). Please. Please tell me the word.

JACOB. I know! We'll play it to him!

KATE (*clapping*). What a lovely idea!

RUPERT. Yes. If you listen closely, cock –

OTHERS. – he'll hear it in the tune!

They warm up. Ugly noises. As they do so they take up positions surrounding him. JOSH *is on the flute.*

MELON *stands waiting. The noise becomes intolerable, but he is evidently attempting to listen intently. Puts his fingers to his ears, lets out a wail.*

They stop playing.

KATE (*gently*). What is it, what's the matter?

MELON. I didn't hear it , didn't hear the word. Just an ugly noise. That's all.

KATE. Of course you didn't, darling. We didn't play it. We were just warming up. Weren't we?

OTHERS. That's right, darling. Just warming up.

KATE. Now listen. Listen and you'll hear.

KATE *leads the others in an at first thin rendition of the 'Ode to joy' from Beethoven's Ninth. Or something choric, equally magnificent. Gradually the chorus fills the theatre, becoming magnificently amplified. The key word in whatever chorus is chosen is replaced by the word 'cuckold'. The* OTHERS, *while continuing to play, though drowned out by the music around, join in the chorus, which climaxes in 'cuckold' again and again as:*

MELON, *appalled, breaks out of the circle, runs across stage to psychiatric room, collapses in chair, sits shaking.*

As MELON *recovers himself, the* OTHERS *pack up their musical instruments, laughing, chattering among themselves,* MELON *watching them occasionally. During the course of his next speech, first* JACOB, *then* MICHAEL, *their instruments packed, go to kiss* KATE *goodbye, salute* MELON *across stage, who salutes back.* JOSH *then exits discreetly. Finally* RUPERT, *his instrument packed, goes over to* KATE, *raises her hand to his lips, then kisses her on cheek, salutes* MELON, *suddenly spots the Sir Archibald book, comes back to table, picks it up, flourishes it across stage at* MELON *as if to say 'nearly forgot' and as* MELON *gestures contemptuously, exits.* KATE *then leaves the room, and as* MELON *nears end of speech,* KATE *comes through door of en suite bathroom, sits down at dressing-table, starts brushing her hair voluptuously.*

MELON. That was the nightmare, you see. That came again and again and again. Recurring, in other words. Yes, my recurring nightmare, that they virtually promised me I wouldn't be having any more as it was a part of my condition, pre-condition as a matter of fact, because I started having it before I — I became, actually went — had my — and yet it's still there, waiting, ready to spring, even in daylight, when I'm fully conscious, trying to organize my experience for prosperity. (*Thinks.*) Posterity. (*Little laugh.*) Could any nightmare be clearer in its meaning? Can there be any problem of interpretation? I always understood it perfectly easily — that I was frightened and ashamed of the world thinking of me as a cuckold. A straight up and down, almost simple-minded

nightmare about one's most basic terror. As it turns out.
Because I didn't know it was my most basic terror until I had
it. And was terrified by it. It taught me — taught me - my
deepest terror. I thank it. But do you know one of them, two
of them, one or two of them, actually refused to accept it on
its own terms. Insisted it must mean something else. Because
dreams and nightmares always mean something else. Even
when they clearly mean exactly what they mean, they mean
something else. One of them actually said that it was just my
version of the usual bomb nightmare. My particular and
personal nightmare about the end of the world. And he said
that my setting it to music meant that something in me was
celebrating — yes, he dared to say my nightmare was a
celebration of the end of the world, a celebration of the bomb
itself. Of course, I tried to explain my position — that I am
absolutely and totally one hundred per cent, without
qualification or reservation, deeply, with every cell of my
body, from the very fibre of my being, against it. Except
possibly as a deterrent. Isn't that the position of any man,
especially a completely sane one? Of course it's true — it's true
that something terrible began to happen which wouldn't have
happened if he hadn't put the idea into my head.

As he speaks once KATE *is established in bed, he crosses to his
sitting-room, passes through the invisible wall, still addressing
the audience.*

Moments when I had a spasm of — of — at the thought of its
being — our being — one day all of us being — (*Going to
bedroom, hesitating as he finishes.*) And to be able to do all
that with a finger! Particularly my suffering! With a finger!
So — yes — I rejoiced. Rejoiced! How could I not? Given how
great my suffering was. (*Goes towards bedroom.*)

*The 'cuckold' chorus, hideously distorted, plays again as he
goes to bedroom.*

MELON (*suavely*), Ah. So you're up here.

KATE. Where else did you think I'd be?

MELON. Well, I didn't know. One moment we were together
    downstairs, the next you'd vanished as if there were

somewhere or someone — darling.

KATE. Love.

MELON. What?

KATE. Love. You call me love. I call you darling.

MELON. Oh. Yes, well perhaps it's time for some changes around
here, eh, love? Darling! Darling! Of course!

KATE *looks at him.*

He calls you darling. Doesn't he? That's why you objected —
you want to keep us distinct. I'm love. He's darling.

KATE. No. I'm love. You're darling. My objection was that you'd
got you and me the wrong way around. Nothing to do with
him at all.

MELON. What do you call him?

KATE (*after a pause, quietly*). I'm not telling you.

MELON. Why not?

KATE. Too personal. Part of your rules —

MELON. Bugger the rules! Bugger the rules! I've scrapped them.
They're gone for good. There are no more rules. All right?

KATE (*watching him*). All right. No more rules.

MELON. So tell me who he is.

KATE. Why?

MELON. Because I want to know, obviously.

KATE. Why?

MELON. I need to know. Need to. I promise — I promise it won't
make any difference to anything. That's a promise, love.

KATE. If it won't make any difference to anything, you can't
really need to know. Can you?

MELON. Let me put it this way, love. My not knowing is
beginning to make a difference. Festering in me all day. That
nightmare that keeps coming back. I can't stand the festering
days and that nightmare at night. I've lost my — my
equilibrium. Knowing will restore it. My equilibrium. The

status quo. Once I know I'll — I'll be myself again. You see? (*Little pause.*) It is someone I know, isn't it? Someone I know well. Isn't it? Possibly even a friend. Is it?

KATE. Possibly, yes.

MELON. You must tell me that much. Just that much. Nothing more if you don't want to. But that much, at least. Please.

KATE (*thinks*). Very well. Yes. A friend. Of a sort.

MELON. Did he begin as a friend before becoming your — bloke?

KATE *nods slightly.*

An old friend of yours? Or of mine?

KATE *says nothing.*

But any old friend of yours is an old friend of mine. Unless you've got an old friend you've always kept quiet about tucked up your sleeve. Have you?

KATE *says nothing.*

So what you're saying — you're actually saying — is that he's an old friend of mine. One of my old friends. One of my oldest friends. That's what you're really saying. Isn't it?

KATE. I'm not saying anything.

MELON. But is he?

KATE. I'm not saying.

MELON. Why not?

KATE. Because it wouldn't be right.

MELON. Not right? Why not?

KATE. It would be treacherous. I won't let you make me be treacherous.

MELON. To him! Treacherous to him!

KATE *looks at him.*

(*Comes over to her.*) Tell me! You tell me! I'll make you tell me, you bitch. Oh please — please tell me! (*Stops.*) Of course! It's Michael, isn't it? Michael! You've always thought him attractive — fancied him. It's Michael. (*Pause.*) Tell me!

At some point during the above, lights have gone on, low, in the sitting-room. JOSH is lying on the sofa, watching television, with earphones. He has a bowl of cornflakes beside him.

MELON reels into the sitting-room, not noticed by JOSH, steadies himself when he sees JOSH, goes to drinks, pours himself a huge one, lights a cigarette, slumps into a chair. Stares at JOSH malevolently.

MELON, after a moment, barks like a dog. JOSH, vaguely aware, turns, sees MELON, takes off earphones.

JOSH. I didn't know you smoked.

MELON. I've been smoking since I was forty-seven and a half. I.e., for the last three weeks. But you could hardly expect yourself to notice. As your head is usually that way — (*Points to screen.*) and not this way. (*Points to self.*) What's that?

JOSH. What?

MELON. That. That you're eating.

JOSH. Cornflakes.

MELON. I thought cornflakes were for breakfast.

   JOSH mutters something.

   What? (*Dangerously.*) What did you say?

JOSH. I said, well, yes.

MELON. To what?

JOSH. To cornflakes being for breakfast.

MELON. But it's nearly seven o'clock. In the evening. What we have outside this house is twilight. Not dawn. They're different things. Almost opposites in some respects. So why are you eating cornflakes at twilight when according to your own statement you take them for breakfast, which everybody knows follows on somewhere between dawn and — midday, in your case, eh? (*Little pause.*) Eh?

JOSH. I've only just got up.

MELON. Why?

JOSH. Didn't get to sleep all night.

MELON. Why, something good on television? Thinking too deeply? Playing with your Jap. Yourself? What? I'm waiting.

JOSH (*in a mutter*). Lot of noise.

MELON. Indeed? What sort of noise?

JOSH (*shrugs*). From your bedroom. You and mum talking, I suppose.

MELON. Suppose? What do you mean suppose? Who else would you expect to hear in our bedroom talking but me and mum, eh?

JOSH. Well, nobody.

MELON. As a matter of interest — have you ever heard anybody but me talking with mum in our bedroom?

JOSH. Well — only the cleaning woman.

MELON (*thoughtfully*). The cleaning woman? Has it ever crossed your mind that she might be — lesbian?

JOSH. Who?

MELON. The cleaning woman.

JOSH *shakes his head.*

Why not? Stranger things.

JOSH. Well, she's a granny, isn't she?

MELON. Nonsense. She's young and black, pretty and enlightened. One knows the type. Active. Radical. Gay rights. Possibly a dyke. Why not?

JOSH. That was the one before last. The student. Filling in.

MELON (*looks at JOSH suspiciously, catches image on screen*). Oh Christ — just look at him! Turn it up.

RUPERT (*on television*). — not only one of our most distinguished military historians, but now, as it turns out, an autobiographer of exceptional modesty, charm and wit. I talked to Sir Archibald in the garden of his Surrey home, about the vicissitudes of his career, and more personally, about the 'fruitful harmony' as he describes it, of his long marriage.

MELON. Fruitful harmony! Hah. In a minute he'll be grovelling to the dog, turn him down, the stupid bugger —

JOSH *turns sound down, gets up.*

Where are you going?

JOSH. Nowhere. (*Shrugs.*) To get an apple.

MELON: 'Nowhere', to get an apple. So that's where you think apples come from, do you, 'nowhere'. I suppose you think that that's where the food in the fridge, the clothes on your back, the money in your pocket come from too, eh? The modern youth's version of it's all growing on trees, eh, 'nowhere'. How appropriate as it's even stupider and vaguely nasty but still justifies your taking as much as you want whenever you want it, well, grasp this, grasp this, it comes from me, I provide it, I work to provide it, I'm a great worker, that's why I'm a great provider, I provide evening cornflakes for my son, and apples at dawn for my son, and friends for my wife and my wife for my friends, so sit down — sit down — and you bloody well answer my question.

JOSH (*sits down*). What question?

MELON. Who is it?

JOSH. Who's what?

MELON (*almost beside himself. Brings himself under control*). All right. Let's begin from the top. Has any of my friends — anyone you know I know — anyone at all — been in this house alone with your mother? Eh? Ever?

JOSH. Alone?

MELON. Yes.

JOSH. I — I don't know.

MELON. Don't know! What sort of answer is that? Apart from being a shifty one.

JOSH. Well, I mean — if they were in the house alone — I wouldn't know, would I? Because I wouldn't be there. That's all — I — I —

MELON. Very well, smarty pants, (*Hurling himself towards*

JOSH, *to hit him. Stops suddenly bewildered.*) I'm sorry. Oh Josh, I'm sorry, sorry, sorry. I — I — you see, I need help. If I could just — answer the question — that one question — I'd be all right again. I know I would. Nothing bad will happen to anyone. I promise. If you — if you can help me. Will you try? (*He is nearly in tears.*)

JOSH *nods.*

Have you ever found anyone in the house with your mother?

JOSH *thinks.*

I mean — like — well, Michael, for instance?

JOSH. Only — when you've been here. Once or twice a few minutes before. That's all.

MELON *studies him suspiciously.*

And that gay friend of yours. He was here once or twice. Crying. And that old guy from the office, he came round once with some stuff for you, and had coffee —

MELON *shakes his head.*

And him of course. (*Points to TV screen.*)

MELON *glances at screen. On it* RUPERT, SIR ARCHIBALD, *the dog.* RUPERT *is addressing dog, in an obsequious manner.* SIR ARCHIBALD *watching dotingly.*

MELON (*barks out a laugh*). There. I told you he'd grovel to the dog. Turn him down. Thank you, Josh. You're being very — very helpful. And kind. I'm going through an odd patch at the moment. Bit like an illness in some respects. So I need — need humouring —

During this RUPERT *has turned back to* SIR ARCHIBALD, *has picked up book that features in* MELON's *nightmare scene, has begun to talk.*

MELON. Anybody else? Anybody at all (*Eyes go to screen. He stares at it, realization dawning.*)

KATE *enters, carrying briefcase, which she puts down both wearily and warily, watching* MELON *as* MELON *continues to gaze at* RUPERT *on screen.*

MELON. There! (*Pointing.*) There! Do you see — do you *see* what he's doing? In front of millions — millions. Look at him, telling me — showing me. In front of millions. Wagging it right in my face — oh, the bugger! The bugger!

KATE *and* JOSH *exchange glances.*

MELON *turning as:*

RUPERT *in the garden fades out on screen into a new item:* RUPERT *snout to snout with a pig.*

MELON (*lets out a roar of laughter*). Now look at him — found the perfect mate! Oh, sorry, love, no offence — no offence, eh? Hah! Let me get you — let me get you a drink.

KATE. No thanks. I don't really feel in the mood —

MELON *goes to bar. Lets out another laugh as he makes* KATE'*s drink.*

KATE (*to* JOSH): How was school?

MELON. Didn't go. Had to catch up on his sleep, poor old chap. Our fault, love. Chattering away at all hours about — (*Lets out another laugh.*) but don't worry, I'm all right, I'm fine now, myself again, yes Melon is himself again — all is light. And sense. Soon it'll be harmony too, I trust, what was the phrase Josh, for Sir Archibald, 'fruitful harmony' — yes, that was it. Here, love — (*Walks towards* KATE *with drink, swerves on impulse towards* JOSH. *Stares into his face.*)

JOSH *stares back, uneasy.*

KATE. Can I have it please? (*Comes over, takes drink from* MELON, *who turns towards her, abstracted.*) I thought you were going over to Yaki's this evening, darling.

JOSH. Um — right. Yes. (*Hurries out.*)

KATE. Why were you looking at Josh like that?

MELON. Just a thought. Of the sort that chaps in my position are prone to. I'd hate to think I'd been fathering old Rupe's son all these years. As well as being (*Swallows.*) cuckolded by him, eh?

KATE. What makes you think he's done either?

MELON. He's just announced it on television.

KATE. That he and I are having an affair. (*Nods.*)

MELON. Oh, he didn't know he was announcing it. I was the only one who could have picked it up. *You* wouldn't have got it even, love.

KATE. A few days ago it was Michael. You've even suspected Jake —

MELON. But I've finally nailed Rupert.

KATE. Well, why not Rupert? (*Laughs.*)

MELON. It just went through me, zip, zip, zip. Like that. Didn't even have to work it out. (*Taps his head.*) A series of lightning steps. And pictures. Yes, that's the point. Pictures too, love.

KATE. Pictures of Rupert and myself — (*Shudders.*)

MELON. No, no, not at all. Much cleverer than that. Much. That Tuesday evening when it all began that Thursday. There they were. Jake first. He picked it up, looked at it, put it down. Then Michael came, picked it up, looked at it, put it down. Then Rupert came. Ignored it. Then remembered it just as he was leaving. Picked it up. And left with it.

KATE. Left with what?

MELON. The Sir Archibald, of course. But don't you see? It was here when he arrived. That's the point. That's the point, love. It was here when he arrived. And he remembered it when he left. *So he'd already been before. Earlier that afternoon.* But forgot to take Sir Archibald with him. That was his mistake. But *remembered* to take it when he left the second time when he was pretending to leave the first time. That was his mistake too. That's why Sir Archibald insisted on turning up in my nightmare. My nightmare understood. It kept trying to tell me — so when I saw him just now, wagging Sir Archibald at me, right in my face, it all came together, zip, zip, zip. Lateral thinking! Rupert. Q.E.D.

KATE. Q.E.D.

MELON. It is Rupert. Isn't it?

KATE. And if I said no —

MELON. You'd be lying. Kate, my love, now I know it's Rupert, I *know* it's Rupert. Rupert is your bloke as — as I'm your husband. As surely as that.

KATE. And there's nothing surer than that. Is there?

MELON. Just say it then. Then we'll be finished. It's all I've ever wanted. Just to know. That's all.

KATE. But you say you do know.

MELON. I still need you to say it, love. Then we can all rest.

KATE. It's Rupert.

MELON. Thank you. (*Kisses her.*) Thank you.

KATE (*after a pause*). I'll go and have my bath —

MELON. Yes. Right. You know the odd thing — the thing I find odd, is your coming here. To do it. Given his sumptuous flat in Highgate. I'd have thought that would be more — more private. In a sense.

KATE (*after a little pause*). I usually didn't have time. To go up to Highgate and back.

MELON (*nodding*). With your heavy schedule. So how often would you say you did it here then, love? In our home? Roughly?

KATE. Not that often.

MELON. Well — how often is not that often, love?

KATE. Once. Sometimes twice.

MELON. A week?

KATE *nods.*

MELON. Once or twice a week for eight years. Well, let's see, that's — that's (*Takes out pocket calculator, works it.*) fifty two or a hundred and four times a year, which means an aggregate of four hundred and sixteen or eight hundred and thirty two times — seems quite often to me, love. Quite often enough. In our bed?

KATE. No.

MELON. Where then?

KATE. Down here.

MELON. Down here. (*Looking around.*) On the sofa? (*Looking at it.*)

KATE. The floor. As a matter of fact.

MELON (*looks at the floor*). Bit rough on the shoulders, I'd have thought.

KATE *says nothing.*

MELON. Eh, love?

KATE. He didn't mind.

MELON. *He* didn't —

KATE. Neither of us did.

MELON. Tuesdays. Did you always do it before our Tuesdays?

KATE. It depended which evening we held them on.

MELON. But when on Tuesday?

KATE *nods.*

Or Thursday?

KATE *half nods.*

MELON. And then he'd go away. And then he'd come back again. Always last. First and last, and I'd ask him who he'd been fucking — (*Looks at her.*)

KATE. We agreed that once you knew. You said that once you knew — we'd rest.

MELON. That was before I knew it was Rupert.

KATE. No. It was immediately after you knew it was Rupert.

MELON. But before I'd understood what it was to know that it was Rupert. Anybody else — any other man — but why him? A man I've always made fun of, that you knew I despised. Was it to humiliate me that you took Rupert? Of all men.

KATE. I took him — I took him —

MELON. Well?

KATE. Because he was proud to have me. And that made me

proud. And that he could be jealous. That made me proud, too.

MELON. Jealous? And are you proud that I'm jealous now?

KATE *shakes her head.*

Why not?

KATE. Because it's too late, I suppose. If you'd been jealous eight years ago —

MELON. Are you, by any chance, confessing that – that you *love* him?

Very faintly, the sounds of the 'cuckold' chorus.

KATE. I'm not confessing anything.

MELON. But not more? Not more than you love me?

KATE *says nothing.*

Answer me! You must answer me! More! Do you love him more!

KATE *exits.*

MELON (*shouting after her, the 'cuckold' chorus growing as he speaks*). Tell me. You must tell me. That's all I want to know. Do you love him more? What sort of things did you do together? In his bed? On our floor? Or did you use his floor too? Did you come to prefer the floor? Did you go to restaurants? Hotels? In the afternoon? How many people saw you? How many people know? Who have you told? Who has he told? Does everybody know? Am I the only one — am I the last — the last — am I? Am I? Just answer that one question. That's all I ask! Do you love him more? More? Oh God, oh God — (*Throws himself to the floor, begins to roll around on it, in an agony, as the 'cuckold' chorus builds to a climax, then stops.*)

MELON *continues to roll around the floor, wailing faintly.*

JOSH *enters, carrying a banana, which he is peeling. Sees MELON, stops.*

MELON *comes to a stop, on his hands and knees, stares at JOSH.*

JOSH. Dad. Dad. Are you all right? (*Makes to go to him.*)

KATE (*enters quickly. Wearing a coat*). Darling. Go and — and —
go. Everything's going to be — (*Gestures.*)

MELON (*getting up*). Josh —

KATE (*looks at* JOSH). Please, darling.

   JOSH *exits*.

KATE. How could you do that? In front of Josh?

MELON. I couldn't help it. I didn't mean to.

KATE. You didn't go to the office then?

MELON. Yes. But I had to come home. You see, I assaulted him.

KATE. Rupert?

MELON. No, no, not Rupert. It was at the office. Old Bore. And
Old Nuisance. Old Gladstone. You see, I thought he was
singing at me that I'm a cuckold. Though really he was singing
cuckoo. Lorde sing cuckoo. Not — cuckold. It was a
misunderstanding. That's all.

KATE. But you assaulted him?

MELON. And — and then did the other thing. Around the floor.
(*Looks at her bewildered.*) How can this be? How can it be?
That I'm not myself, love?

KATE. Do you want a drink? (*Goes to drinks*).

MELON. How was your — your day?

KATE. Hard. A hard day. (*Fixing drinks.*)

MELON. Oh. And did you see him?

KATE. No.

MELON. Are you lying, love?

KATE. Yes.

MELON. So you saw him?

KATE. No.

MELON. But you said you were lying.

KATE (*brings him his drink*). I was lying when I said that.

MELON. That you hadn't seen him?

KATE. No. That I was lying.

MELON. Why?

KATE. Because there isn't any truth any more except your truth.
So it doesn't matter whether I saw him or didn't see him,
whether I say I saw him or say I didn't see him. Your truth is
that I saw him. So whatever I say is a lie. To one of us.

MELON. And did you — did you make love?

KATE. No. We tried to. The police moved us on. I thought for a
moment we were going to be clamped, but they let us off with
a caution.

MELON. Why are you punishing me, why? Is it because you've
stopped loving me?

KATE. I'm not punishing you. I'm coping. That's what I'm doing.
Coping.

MELON. Have you stopped loving me? Please say.

KATE (*after a small pause*). I don't know.

MELON. But you have loved me.

KATE *nods*.

MELON. And did you mind — all the time — about my little
sexual — sexual — (*Gestures.*) is that it?

KATE. I couldn't spend the rest of my life minding about your
infidelities, could I, if you were going to spend the rest of
yours being unfaithful?

MELON. But you knew they were casual. I've never stopped
loving you. Never. Even when I knew *you* were unfaithful. I've
loved you more and more. That's why I didn't mind —

KATE. But you did mind. You enjoyed minding. Minding was
your itch. Which you scratched and scratched, remember. It
was an aphrodisiac. It made me more and more desirable —
you used to say.

MELON. It isn't desire I want now. It's love. I'm like this because
I no longer believe you love me. So you must. Please. Love me.

KATE. I'll try. I've always tried, you know. To love you.

MELON. I don't want you to try. I hate the thought of you trying. I want you to come back to me and be. My loving Kate. Please.

KATE (*after a pause, wearily*). I'll do my best.

MELON. Your best?

KATE. Yes.

MELON. Do your best? Oh God — (*Falls to the floor, begins to roll about briskly, as a snatch of the 'cuckold' chorus plays. The music stops.* MELON *gets to his hands and knees.*)

KATE (*after a moment*). I do wish — I do wish you'd get up. We've both always hated the idea of having a dog in the house. (*Attemps to laugh.*)

MELON (*reaching up a hand*). Please help me. What am I going to do, love? Please help me.

KATE. I will. If you come with me.

MELON (*looking up at her suspiciously*). Where to?

KATE. To see someone who might be able to help.

MELON. I want to go out. With you. Take me out. Let's see friends. Or have dinner. Just the two of us.

KATE. We can't do that. We can't inflict you on our friends and then have you roll about their floors. Not any more. It isn't fair on them. Or on the restaurants. People might think it's the food. The chefs' reputations —

MELON. You're very hard. You've become very hard.

KATE. You've worn me down until only my hard bits are left.

MELON. Love me. That's all I ask. I beg. Love me.

KATE. I can't. I'm sorry, I can't. At least at the moment.

MELON. Oh try. Please try. I'll do anything.

KATE. But will you do it on your feet?

MELON. Help me Kate.

KATE. Then come with me. (*Holds out her hand.*) It's our only chance.

MELON, *after a pause, shakes his head, drops to his knees, buries his face in his arms.*

KATE *looks at him, drops her hand, makes to the door.*

MELON, *lifts his head, sees her, scrambles after her on his hands and knees, seizes her hand. Gets up. She looks at him, then holding his hand, leads him towards:*

The psychiatric room on which lights slowly up as MELON *and* KATE *advance towards it.* KATE *leads him into the room, towards the hard-back chair.*

MELON *hesitates, fearful.* KATE *silently, firmly commands him to sit down with a look. Still clasping her hand,* MELON *sits.*

KATE *tries to remove her hand.* MELON *clings to it, desperately.* KATE, *after a short, fierce struggle, gets her hand free. She turns, hurries to the door, as* MELON *rises, stumbles after her.* KATE *exits, walks quickly off, lights out on her.* MELON *continues to door, stares into the darkness, turns, comes back in. Looks at the chair, goes over, sits on it.*

JACOB *enters. Throughout following scene,* MELON *is smoking heavily.*

JACOB. Hello.

MELON. Oh. Hello there. Joshua, isn't it?

JACOB. Jake.

MELON. Jacob. Yes. Well, I knew it was someone biblical. What are you doing here?

JACOB. I'm just passing through. Professionally, so to speak. So I thought I'd look in —

MELON. Ah yes. Yes of course. Checking out your loonies, eh?

JACOB. Yes.

MELON. And how are they doing?

JACOB. How are you doing?

MELON. Oh, rather well, thank you, Jacob, I think. Though to tell you the truth I find thinking very difficult at the moment. I've tried some straightforward consecutive stuff, you know, going from A to -- to -- (*Thinks*.) B. Taking it one step at a time. And back again. But there is a slight tendency for my mind to wander.

JACOB. Between A and B?

MELON. Exactly. That's it. Yes. A kind of wandering between the stretch from A to -- to --

JACOB. B.

MELON. Yes. Such a relief after all that bounding from one -- one passion, is that it?

JACOB. Could be.

MELON. Passion. (*Nods*.) And the great thing is, Jacob, they've filled me full of some wonderful pills. The only problem is I don't know precisely which pill is doing the talking. Thinking. Dreaming. Being. Slow pills, fast pills, right as rain pills, down the drain pills, Jacob, eh? (*Little laugh*.) How are you, Jacob? Everything going all right, still unhappy, I hope. Tell me about it, Jacob.

JACOB. Oh yes, don't worry, nothing much to tell and still unhappy, Mark.

MELON. That's the ticket, Jacob. (*Little pause. Stares blankly, nods*.) That's the ticket. When is -- when is Mate coming to see me?

JACOB. Mate? Oh, you mean Kate.

MELON (*Thinks*). Yes, Kate. My mate, Kate. When is she coming to see me, do you know?

JACOB. I understand you have an understanding. She's not to see you until you're better. In case seeing her makes you worse. Professional decision.

MELON. Ah.

JACOB. And of course she's got her work. The only breadwinner at the moment, so to speak.

MELON. Ah.

JACOB (*gets up*). I'd better be getting along.

MELON. You will come and see me again. Won't you, Jacob?

JACOB. The very next time I have to be here.

MELON. Thank you. And Jacob. Love to — (*Gestures.*)

JACOB. Of course. You used to call me Jake.

MELON. Perhaps — perhaps I've learnt a touch of respect. Eh, Jacob?

JACOB. Respect is calling me Jake.

MELON. Thank you. Thank you. Quite right. Thank you — (*Thinks.*) old chap.

JACOB *exits.*

MELON *sits. Makes to speak. Gestures feebly, falls into a light doze as:*

JOSH *enters.*

MELON (*opens eyes, stares at* JOSH.) Wife not with you? (*Little pause.*)

JOSH. Wife?

MELON. Mine. Your mother. You know.

JOSH (*shakes his head*). She hopes she can come soon.

MELON. How are the A levels coming?

JOSH. They've gone. Been and gone. I didn't do too well.

MELON. Ah. Who cares? (*Looks at* JOSH, *smiles emptily.*) Look at me. Five O levels. Three A levels. First-class honours degree. Better off with two CSE's, eh? Education is — education is — EST. That's what education is. Not CSE but EST.

JOSH. EST? What board is that?

MELON. Electric Shock Treatment. That's what board that is. Electric Shock Treatment.

JOSH. Electric shock? But I thought — I mean, there was a programme on telly just the other night and they said that was a thing of the past.

MELON. Not of my past, Jake. (*Looks at him.*) Josh. They
explained that sometimes shock to the brain can be as — as —
(*Remembering word.*) efficacious as a kick up the arse.
Sometimes more so as it's more sensitive. Though probably
not in my case, one of them said. (*Laughs.*) It was a joke (*Little
pause.*) I think.

JOSH. Oh. (*Laughs. Gets up.*)

He puts a hand fleetingly on MELON's *shoulder, exits.*

MELON *stares after him. Stubs out cigarette. He takes a
cigarette packet out of his pocket, crumples it, throws it into
wastepaper basket. Takes out a fresh packet, opens it, takes
out a cigarette, crumples it, throws it into wastepaper basket,
continues to do this as:*

MICHAEL *enters, busily, carrying a briefcase.*

MELON (*with life*). Michael!

MICHAEL. Mark! (*Sitting down, opening briefcase.*) Everything
all right, you comfortable?

MELON. Oh yes, thank you, Michael, yes. I've been having a lot
of therapy and group analysis and we've been into all the
sibling stuff, you see. You're the brother I never had. That's
why I resented you and wanted to kill you. Because you didn't
exist, you see. So it was your fault really.

MICHAEL *nods.*

And the great thing is they've stopped me smoking. They're
very pleased with that, they've never seen anyone not smoke
as much as I'm not smoking. Look, I must be up to the 200,
300 a day mark. Well done. Well done, Mark Melon, eh,
Michael? (*Little pause.*) And good pills too.

MICHAEL. Well, everything certainly seems (*Looking around
him, looking back at* MELON.) — seems in order.

MELON. Oh it is. And how good of you to come and see me. I
was sure you would. In the end. Has Kate mentioned when she
might — might um —

MICHAEL. I've only spoken to her once or twice on the 'phone
— very briefly as she's in the middle of a big new production, I

gather, quite prestigious — now, here, if you'd initial each of these. (*Putting a pile of documents on* MELON's *lap, pen into his hand.*)

MELON (*automatically begins to initial*). What are they, exactly?

MICHAEL. Oh, a few legal and technical matters — you know — the nature of your contract makes it difficult to organize certain things without your consent — we can't even commission or authorize publication — of course nobody envisaged that you'd ever be away — and certainly not this long.

MELON, *during this, has taken pocket calculator out, is looking at it hopefully.*

Oh, you won't need that.

MELON. Won't I? (*Disappointed.*) Oh. (*Puts it away.*) Three or four weeks isn't that long, surely? I must say — it's good to have a pen and some documents in my hand again — haven't lost my touch, eh? (*Laughs.*)

MICHAEL. No, you look as you always look.

MELON. Everything's all right at the office, then?

MICHAEL. Oh yes. We're hanging on without you.

MELON. And how are things with Melinda?

MICHAEL. Melissa. We're back together. Really rather happily — virtually for the first time in our marriage.

MELON. Well, Michael — that's — that's — and little Marcus?

MICHAEL. We've sent him to a boarding school. In Canada. We gather that he's beginning to settle down. (*Takes documents from* MELON, *who is beginning, vaguely, to scrutinize them.*)

MELON. Oh. Good. Good.

MICHAEL. I'd better get back. Thanks for these. (*Goes to door.*)

MELON. Tell me — how's — how's old Baldwin. Chamberlain.

MICHAEL. If you mean Gladstone, he's finished at last.

MELON. Finished? Dead, you mean? Oh no!

MICHAEL. No, no, finished his memoirs. We're going to publish them.

MELON. Oh that's — that's —

MICHAEL. Isn't it? (*Goes to door*.) Oh, by the way, Mark, it's been six months.

MELON. Mmmm?

MICHAEL. You've been away six months. Not three or four weeks. (*Exits.*)

RUPERT *enters.*

MELON *stares at* RUPERT, *flinches.*

RUPERT (*kneels*). Our father, which art in Heaven, hallowed be thy name.

MELON *kneels.*

A sacred version of the 'cuckold' chorus plays through this, possibly on an organ.

RUPERT *holds out his arms.*

MELON *moves across on knees into* RUPERT's *arms.*

Thy kingdom come, thy will be done on earth, as it is in Heaven. Give us this day our daily bread. Forgive us our trespasses, as we forgive them that trespass against us. Lead us not into temptation. And deliver us from evil. For thine is the kingdom, the power and the glory. For ever and ever, Amen.

RUPERT *and* MELON *kiss.*

RUPERT *rises, exits.*

MELON *rises, sits on his chair.*

Pause.

KATE *enters, unseen by* MELON.

MELON (*in a dull voice*). On the other hand, I have to concede that I went — was put — under their care in one condition, and emerged in another. Somebody had somehow changed something. Is there anything here to explain? Beyond my continuing resentment that they should exist? Or is my resentment really that there should exist in me a need for them? Is it possible that I might not have emerged without them? It is possible, on the other hand, that if I'd confined myself to a room at home, sipped herbal tea, rolled around the floor for nine months and — and so forth — I might have emerged at the allotted hour — this one — the allotted minute — this one — exactly as I am now. Waiting. Waiting to be redeemed. Like an article in one of those pawn shops that no longer exist. Either. (*Laughs slightly, miserably, then sees* KATE.)

(*After a pause.*) Hello, love.

KATE. It's time for you to come home. (*Puts out a hand.*)

MELON, *his hand trembling, reaches out to her, takes her hand.*

KATE *leads him to the door, and as they exit, lights out on the psychiatric room and as* MELON *and* KATE *step towards it, lights up on* MELON's *sitting-room.*

JOSH, JACOB *waiting.* JOSH *watching television,* JACOB *glancing into a book.*

MELON *and* KATE *enter.*

MELON. Well, here I am. Again. (*Little laugh.*) Jake. Josh. (*Hesitates, kisses him.*)

JOSH *turns off television.*

No, leave it on, more like old times, eh?

JACOB. You look — you look fine, Mark.

MELON. Thanks. Yes. Well, apparently I'll be a bit short on sparkle — takes a bit of time for the juices to run — the prescription is to put a toe in the water — test the temperature — rather than plunging boldly — look well yourself, Jake — everything all right in the surgery and — and other place.

JACOB. Oh, much the same. Patrick's left me. But then I don't expect you knew about Patrick, he's two boys on from when you — (*Gestures.*) So to all intents and purposes, no change really. I'm sorry I didn't get a chance to visit you in the hospital. I tried, once or twice, but they wanted to keep you away from old associations for a time. And then when I could, things got a bit difficult on my side.

MELON. No. No, that's all right — to tell you the truth I'm not clear who did and who didn't. And where those who did really came from. Visits. Or visitations.

JACOB. Well, I'd better —

MELON. No, no, stay a while, have a drink — a drink for Jacob, love. I'll just go and — check around — eh? Right back — (*Exits, as lights fade, but not completely down on* KATE, JOSH, JACOB.)

During the above lights have come up on MELON's *office,* SAMANTHA's *desk empty.* MICHAEL *is standing at* MELON's *desk, turning over pages of typescript.*

MELON *appears, crosses, braces himself, enters office.* MICHAEL *continues working.*

MELON (*after a moment*). Well, here I am.

MICHAEL (*looks up sightlessly, then eventually locates* MELON). Mark! (*Gets up.*) Sorry. Thought you were coming in on Monday. At the top of a week.

MELON. Oh. Well I did say I might look in today — toe in the water — test the temperature — perhaps I — I wasn't very clear. Sorry.

MICHAEL. Not at all. I'd forgotten. Good idea, really. Well — (*Gestures.*) you're back. Who cares on which day? Tuesday or Thursday — Monday or Sunday even.

MELON (*looks around*). Everything looks much the same.

MICHAEL. Except for me, of course. (*Laughs.*)

MELON. You?

MICHAEL. My being in here, your being in there. (*Gestures to door,* MICHAEL's *previous office.*)

MELON. I'm in there?

MICHAEL. Well, if I'm to have your office, you should have mine. Logically.

MELON. I hadn't realized — you're um — um —

MICHAEL. Managing director. Somebody had to be, you know, while you were away. Take over the responsibilities — how else could we function? You agreed. Don't you remember?

MELON. Not quite.

MICHAEL. You signed the papers. Don't you remember?

MELON (*after a moment, nods*). So what shall I do?

MICHAEL. Oh, the kind of stuff I did. Just as I've been doing the kind of stuff you did. We'll work it out. You'll get used to it in no time. And then when you're fully fit, we'll — (*Gestures.*) work it out.

MELON. What happened to Joey? I mean, Danny.

MICHAEL. Sammy. (MELON *nods.*) Got into university. We've got a nice chap on the desk, though. If a little short on cheeriness. Didn't you notice him when you came in? The bald black man from Antigua?

MELON *shakes his head.*

MICHAEL. Oh, he'll be around somewhere. You can generally smell him coming.

MELON. Smell him?

MICHAEL. Yes. Smokes a pipe. A heady brew.

GLADSTONE (*who has been approaching door, knocks, enters*). Michael, you're really going to have to do something about Agnes. I've just spent an hour with her on the 'phone, she seems to think we're going to let her design all the covers of all her reissues as well as the unpublished novels she's written in the last — (*sees* MELON.} Mark? I thought you weren't coming in 'til Monday, wasn't that what we agreed?

MELON. Toe in the water — to test the temperature, um congratulations on the memoirs, Arnold.

GLADSTONE. Yes, isn't it odd, all the interest shown — has Michael told you about the *Sunday Times,* and almost the best thing — from my point of view anyway, is that finishing them at last has given me a new zest, hasn't it, Michael, as your absence meant I had to fairly pitch myself into the fray or goodness knows — so I have you to thank really, Mark. Although of course I don't mean, don't mean —

MICHAEL. You mustn't worry about Agnes, Arnold, Melissa and I are having supper with her tomorrow, and Melissa's becoming very adroit at handling her —

MELON *drifts out of office.*

GLADSTONE. Well, I just pray she isn't going to make a nuisance of herself. (*Goes to cupboard, takes out musical instrument.*)

MICHAEL (*taking a musical instrument out of drawer*). Yes, I must say I sometimes wish Mark hadn't thought up that cookbook for her — but then can't blame him really, nobody could have expected so much fuss —

MICHAEL *and* GLADSTONE *carry on fussy conversation in musical terms, low, on their instruments.*

In drawing-room, JOSH, JAKE, KATE *have taken out musical instruments, are playing in desultory fashion, until* RUPERT *appears on the television screen, playing musical instrument.* KATE *sees him, plays to him. He seems to play back. All this, low. It is a chamber variation on the 'cuckold' chorus.*

MELON. So one day the earth opens at your feet. Or happens to open where your feet happen to be. The next day, or the day after, or nine months later, or never, it closes again. And there one is. On terra firma. Waiting. Watching. Moving slowly and carefully. Because now you know you never know when it's going to open again. And again. And again. So watching and waiting, moving slowly and carefully, taking no offence, trying to give none, avoiding temptation and forgiving trespasses in the hope that yours will be forgiven, being thankful for your daily bread, praying that neither the kingdom nor anything else powerful and glorious will come in your lifetime, but praying that where you stand is where you actually are, that what you see is all that's truly visible, that what you hear is the usual medley of human noises — one step at a time. (*Pause.*) Is what I ask. (*Pause. Begins to play.*) Safe, in other words. Safe and sound. (*Little pause.*) Safe and sane. And so forth.

Gradually, led by MELON, *they play in harmony, without passion or fire — humdrum in fact.*

Lights down.